Insurance Words

and Their Meanings

A Glossary of Property and Casualty Terms

by

Robert W. Strain, CPCU, CLU
Dean
The College of Insurance

and

Eleven Other Authorities

26401

ISBN #0-942326-07-5

Insurance Words
and Their Meanings

Thirteenth Edition, Second Printing
August, 1982

Preface

This dictionary is the product of more than 25 years of work by more than a dozen individuals, each an expert in his chosen field. We hope it will be of help to the student of insurance. It provides quick access to information when it is needed, which is most effective for learning. It offers a compendium of knowledge in capsule form, relieving the reader from lengthy searches for answers. It is kept up-to-date, which makes it useful today. For example, the present edition is completely overhauled from its 1978 version, including many new terms, some of which are:

captive insurance company
cash flow plan
disappearing deficit
discrimination
entitlement, psychology of
ERISA
fiduciary liability insurance
Free Trade Zone
gap coverage
health maintenance
   organization (HMO)
hospice
innocent capacity
insurance exchanges
margin account insurance

monitoring competition
NAIC Insurance Regulatory
   Information System (IRIS)
New York Insurance Exchange
priority company
redlining
residual market mechanism
retention clause
reverse competition
social inflation
sunset provision
take-all-comers
takeover defense insurance
unfair discrimination
usual ranges

Some new reinsurance words have also been taken with permission from *Reinsurance*, 1980, The College of Insurance, from among its 260-word glossary of reinsurance terms.

The first author in 1954 of *Insurance Words and Their Meanings* was the late Vincent L. Gallagher. Mr. Gallagher served in New York as president of the Monarch Fire Insurance Company and U.S. Manager of the Pearl Assurance Company, Ltd., of London. Later he was joined for 12 years by his friend and business associate in the Pearl Group, the late Gerald R. Heath, who maintained the book until his death in 1976. Mr. Heath's business career of 45 years spanned four countries—England, South Africa, Canada, and the United States. At the time of his 1974 retirement in New York, he was vice president of The Monarch Insurance Company of Ohio and the Pearl American Corporation.

Mr. Heath was a staunch supporter of The Insurance Society of New York and served The College of Insurance as chairman of its casualty underwriting advisory course committee. During his residency in Canada, he served as chairman of several committees of the Insurance Institute of Canada, and he was also a Fellow of the Insurance Institute of England. It was his wish that I continue the work that he and Mr. Gallagher had started.

The current edition of this book was prepared with the help of the following consulting experts. All authors are present or former associates at The College of Insurance, either full-time or part-time, serving as professors or administrative staff as their titles indicate. Most of them helped with the 1978 revision. Each person was selected by me for his expertise in a particular discipline (shown above his name), and was responsible for reviewing the terms in that category. On behalf of all who will benefit from their work, I sincerely thank them.

Accounting

REGINALD V. HILL (Adjunct Assistant Professor)
Assistant Comptroller, Royal Insurance
150 William Street, New York, New York 10038

Agency, Brokerage, and Marketing

ALFRED I. JAFFE, CPCU
Associate Professor, The College of Insurance,
123 William Street, New York, New York 10038

Bonding

ROBERT W. SCHMITT, CPCU (Adjunct Assistant Professor)
Assistant Vice President, The Continental Insurance Companies,
80 Maiden Lane, New York, New York 10038

Life and Health

MURRAY ROSEN, CLU
Associate Professor and Chairman,
Life and Health Insurance Division, The College of Insurance,
123 William Street, New York, New York 10038

Property and Liability

GEORGE M. GOTTHEIMER, JR., CPCU, CLU (Adjunct Assistant Professor)
Vice President, John D. Ryan & Co., Inc.,
80 Pine Street, New York, New York 10005

NORMAN HOFFMAN, CPCU
Assistant Professor of Insurance, The College of Insurance,
123 William Street, New York, New York 10038

WILLIAM B. PUGH, JR., LL.B. (Lecturer, NAIC Commissioner Seminar)
Attorney
Penn Valley Road
Media, Penna. 19063

Regulation and Legal Aspects

ROBERT FISHBEIN, LL.B. (Professor and Counsel)
The College of Insurance,
123 William Street, New York, New York 10038

Reinsurance

JEAN F. WEBB, IV, CPCU (Adjunct Assistant Professor)
Vice President, North American Reinsurance Corporation,
245 Park Avenue, New York, New York 10017

Risk Management

MATTHEW LENZ, JR., CPCU, CLU
Assistant to the President and
Chairman of the Property and Liability Insurance Division,
The College of Insurance,
123 William Street, New York, New York 10038

The contributions of two of the above persons stand out because of the extra mile they walked in making the current edition our best effort to date. With the editor, they scrutinized every term in the entire volume. Bill Pugh, in spite of having served as INA's associate general counsel, continues to help many organizations with his extensive knowledge of insurance matters. Norman Hoffman brought, from his earlier background as agent-broker-risk manager, a degree of thoroughness to the work which is the envy of many.

Messrs. Pugh and Hoffman and the nine other contributors have enjoyed working together for this worthy cause. Its compensations have been generous, although limited to psychic income. Its offer of a claim-to-fame has been of dubious value, since insurance lexicographer as a term is not yet recognized by the IRS as a charitable organization. But we console ourselves that we are appreciated out there. Accordingly, we pledge ourselves to remain alert to those insurance developments which matter, and aloof to those which do not, to the end that the reader may yet benefit from another revision. The next one is scheduled for 1984, the year in which Big Brother is expected to be watching over us. If we still have our wits about us then, perhaps this little compendium of insurance terminology may yet refresh us all in the days ahead.

Robert W. Strain

New York City
January 5, 1981

A

ABANDONMENT — 1) In ocean marine insurance, the transfer by the insured to an underwriter of all rights, title, and interest in and to the insured property in return for the sum insured. It is effected by the insured's tender of such transfer (notice of abandonment) and the underwriter's acceptance. A valid tender can be made only when the facts show that there has been a "constructive total loss" of the insured property through an insured peril. In such case, however, the insured can recover the sum insured as for a total loss, even though the underwriter has refused to accept the tender and there has been no "abandonment." 2) The word also appears in "sue and labor" clauses of various inland marine policies by way of a stipulation that compliance with the requirements of the clause shall be without prejudice to either the insured or the insurer respecting waiver or acceptance of "abandonment." 3) In fire insurance, abandonment is relinquishing ownership of damaged property to an insurer to permit a total loss claim to be made, but both the Standard Fire Policy and the Homeowners Policy prohibit such abandonment. Instead, such policies require the insured to protect damaged property from further loss.

ACCEPT — The taking of risk (by an underwriter or other person authorized to act) by expressing a willingness to issue insurance.

ACCIDENT — An event or occurrence which is unintended, unforeseen and unexpected. Something which could not be considered as a foreseeable occurrence and consequence of an undertaking; a casualty or mishap.

ACCIDENT INSURANCE — Insurance covering death, dismemberment, or loss of sight, loss of income, and medical expenses caused by accidental injury.

ACCIDENT PREVENTION — All the ways and means used to avoid the occurrence of an accident or to reduce its consequences if it does occur: the control of personal performance, machine performance, and physical environment, including the training needed to reduce the number of accidents and cost of accidental injuries. Accident prevention is one of the less publicized functions of risk managers and insurers, many of which improve safety in industry, the home, and on the roads through safety engineering and research. Also known as LOSS PREVENTION.

ACCIDENT & SICKNESS INSURANCE — See HEALTH INSURANCE.

ACCIDENT YEAR EXPERIENCE — Simplistically, the statistical matching of all losses occurring (regardless of when the losses are reported) during a given 12 month period of time, with all premium earned (regardless of when the premium was written) during the same period of time. Calendar year experience, on the other hand, simplistically is the statistical matching of all losses incurred (not necessarily occurring) within a given 12 month period, usually beginning on January 1, with all premium earned within the same period of time. Yet a third related term is policy year experience, which simplistically is the statistical segregation of all premiums and losses attributable to policies having an inception or renewal date within a given 12 month period.

ACCIDENTAL MEANS — The cause of a result which was not intentional.

ACCOMMODATION LINE — A line an underwriter accepts which does not meet all or most criteria but which is accepted for other reasons: a) the value of the total account, the producer, or the center of influence; b) to help a good producer, and thus possibly get more business from him or her.

ACCOUNT CURRENT — A monthly report by an agent to the insurance company including policy numbers, premiums, and applicable commissions on business produced by that agent.

ACCOUNTANTS LIABILITY INSURANCE — A form of professional liability insurance covering the negligence of accountants in their professional practices.

ACCOUNTS RECEIVABLE INSURANCE — Coverage which protects businesses against their inability to collect their accounts receivable because of the loss of supporting records.

ACQUISITION COST — 1) The cost of selling insurance. Normally the agent's and broker's commission, but in some cases the term is used to designate any cost of putting the business on the books. 2) In rate filings by insurers with state insurance departments, one of three expense elements shown: general expenses, commissions, and other acquisition costs (such as advertising and service office expenses).

ACT OF GOD — An event beyond human origin or control. Lightning, windstorms, and earthquakes are examples, the damage from which would not be the responsibility of a bailee, although the bailee might be responsible for many other calamities. Acts of God are excluded by the usual bill of lading as well as by some insurance policies, unless specifically included.

ACTUAL CASH VALUE — The basis of loss settlement in property insurance policies, which takes into consideration such factors as replacement value less depreciation, market value, rental value, the use of the building, the area in which it is located, obsolescence, assessed valuation and any other factor which would have an effect upon the value. A working rule-of-thumb definition, however, is "replacement cost new at the time of loss, less depreciation." See REPLACEMENT COST VALUE.

ACTUARY — A social mathematician who uses mathematical skills to define, analyze and solve complex business and social problems involving insurance and employee benefit programs. The work of actuaries involves the various contingencies which face human beings: birth, marriage, sickness, accident, loss of property, legal liability, retirement and death, and the financial effects which these and other contingencies have on various insurance and benefit programs. Many of these programs involve long-range financial obligations, for which actuarial forecasts are fundamental in maintaining a sound financial basis: rate-making, premium and loss reserving, investment valuation, pension benefits, and insurance statistics, among others.

ADDITIONAL INSURED — A person, other than the named insured, who is protected by the terms of the policy. Usually a specified individual such as a spouse or a member of the insured's family—but sometimes, as in automobile insurance, any person provided that person is driving the insured vehicle with the insured's permission.

ADDITIONAL LIVING EXPENSE INSURANCE — Insurance for the extra amount it costs an insured to live until repairs are made to the insured's dwelling.

ADJACENT — One building is adjacent to another if it is very close to another building with no intervening building.

ADJOINING —- When a building is so located that it touches another.

ADJUSTABLE POLICY — A policy in which the exposure basis is a variable (such as sales or payroll), which can only be determined at the end of the policy term. See AUDIT, REPORTING POLICY.

ADJUSTER — One who determines the amount of loss suffered. A "company" or "independent" adjuster represents the company. A "public" adjuster represents the policyholder.

ADJUSTMENT — The process of determining the amount of a loss and agreeing on the amount with the claimant who has suffered the loss.

ADJUSTMENT BUREAU — An organization which maintains a staff of adjusters and whose business it is to adjust losses for those companies which refer their losses to the bureau. See GENERAL ADJUSTMENT BUREAU.

ADMINISTRATOR — A person appointed by the court to administer a decedent's estate where there is no will, where the executor is unable to act, or where the will named none.

ADMIRALTY COURTS — Section of the federal or national court system which deals with matters pertaining to vessels, crew, and their cargoes navigating on interstate or international waters. Maritime procedures, precedents and rules are different in admiralty courts than in other courts.

ADMITTED ASSETS — Those assets, or portions thereof, of an insurance company which under state insurance laws may be taken into account in establishing the financial condition of the insurance company, e.g., agents' balances or uncollected premiums under 90 days old. See NONADMITTED ASSETS.

ADMITTED COMPANY — A foreign or alien insurance company which has been licensed by the insurance department of the state in question, and thereby is authorized to conduct business within that state to the extent licensed.

ADMITTED MARKET — See ADMITTED COMPANY.

AD VALOREM — In marine insurance cargo and protection and indemnity policies, high valued cargoes such as specie, bullion, negotiable documents, jewels, etc.

ADVANCE PREMIUM — A provisional or deposit premium charged at the start of a policy term, with the final premium determined after the policy has expired.

ADVERSE SELECTION — The insuring of one or more risks with a higher chance of loss than that contemplated by the applicable insurance rate. The selection of such risks is adverse because the rate is inadequate.

ADVERTISERS LIABILITY INSURANCE — Covers an insured against claims for libel, slander, defamation, infringement of copyright, invasion of privacy, etc., arising out of its advertising program. Also available for radio and television stations and advertising agencies.

ADVISORY ORGANIZATION — One of the three basic forms of insurance organizations: rating bureaus, advisory organizations, and trade associations. Rating bureaus make and file rates, rating plans, schedules, manuals and forms for members, subscribers and service purchasers who choose to use them. Advisory organizations perform

8

advisory functions for insurers relative to these rating bureau activities and, like rating bureaus, are licensed by state insurance departments and subject to examination and other regulation. Trade associations are cooperative organizations to protect the business interests of their member insurers, producers, adjusters, attorneys, or other groups. Either a rating bureau or an advisory association can function as a statistical organization, and the function of advisory organizations and trade associations can overlap. Distinctions in functions can best be appreciated by understanding that, historically, rating and advisory organizations were licensed and regulated under state rating laws because of the public interest in the cooperative activities of insurers, relative to pricing and the need for regulation, in order to replace application of antitrust laws. See RATING BUREAU.

AFTER CHARGE — In certain fire insurance rating schedules for commercial property, certain additions or loadings on the rate are made for defects (such as poor housekeeping or minor wiring defects) which can be easily corrected. The purpose of separate charges for such defects is to encourage their correction promptly, in which event the rate will be lowered by the amount of the after charges.

AGENCY PLANT — A company's sales organization.

AGENCY SUPERINTENDENT — A management position of an insurance company usually having supervision over a territorial division and the agents therein. Often strictly a production person, as distinguished from one in charge of certain lines of insurance.

AGENT — One who has the authority to act for another. In insurance language, an agent is the person who sells insurance by contacting the policyholder, and by contract and by law is endowed with many of the powers of the company itself. See INDEPENDENT AGENT, EXCLUSIVE AGENT, and BROKER.

AGENTS QUALIFICATION LAWS — Laws which define standards of insurance knowledge which an individual who may be licensed as an agent must meet.

AGGREGATE EXCESS OF LOSS REINSURANCE — See STOP LOSS REINSURANCE.

AGGREGATE LIMIT — In a policy providing such an aggregate limit, the maximum amount the insurer will pay during the policy period, irrespective of the policy's limit of liability. See LIMIT OF LIABILITY.

AGREED AMOUNT CLAUSE — A condition of a policy stating that the insurer agrees to waive the coinsurance requirement in consideration of the insured's maintaining insurance equal to the amount agreed upon at the inception of the policy.

AGRICULTURAL EQUIPMENT FLOATER — An inland marine policy tailored to insure the equipment found on a farm or ranch. Available on an "all-risks" or "named perils" basis.

AIR CARGO LIABILITY INSURANCE — Coverage for the legal liability of an air carrier for loss or damage to cargo while in its care, custody or control.

AIRCRAFT HULL INSURANCE — Covers any loss arising out of physical damage to the aircraft itself in flight, on the ground, or both.

AIRCRAFT LIABILITY INSURANCE — Covers the insured for both bodily injury and property damage liability arising out of the ownership or use of the insured aircraft.

AIRCRAFT PASSENGER LIABILITY INSURANCE — Covers the liability resulting from bodily injury and sickness or disease suffered by any passenger arising out of the ownership or use of the insured aircraft.

AIRCRAFT PRODUCT LIABILITY INSURANCE — Coverage required by a manufacturer of aircraft, components or equipment. Also those involved in selling aircraft, parts, or fuel, or engaged in repair or maintenance of aircraft. This policy protects these various parties against claims arising from injury or damage caused by defects in the products sold or manufactured or from improperly completed operations.

AIRPORT LIABILITY INSURANCE — Covers the liability arising out of the ownership or maintenance of premises, normally a hangar located at either a municipal or private airport.

ALARM VALVE — A mechanism on many automatic sprinkler systems which activates an alarm, sometimes a loud gong, or in other cases signals directly to the fire department when a sprinkler head has opened.

ALIEN COMPANY — An insurance company incorporated in a country outside the U. S., but conducting business within the U. S.

ALL AMERICAN MARINE SLIP — A syndicate of many American insurance and reinsurance companies formed in 1972 to provide a substantial market for large, high-risk or unusual marine exposures historically handled by foreign markets.

ALL-COMERS — See TAKE-ALL-COMERS.

ALL-RISK POLICY — A policy which covers loss caused by any peril which is not excluded, as contrasted to "named peril" policies which protect against certain perils named in the policies. Usual to certain types of property and marine insurance contracts, the term

10

"all risk" frequently appears in quotes, since such coverage includes "almost" all risks (e.g., all but those excluded).

ALLIANCE OF AMERICAN INSURERS — A trade association of primarily mutual property and casualty insurers, though as of September, 1977, membership was open to non-mutual companies. Fosters research and publishes educational materials, with headquarters in Chicago. Formerly the American Mutual Insurance Alliance.

ALLIED LINES — Those coverages which are frequently written with property insurance (e.g., sprinkler leakage, earthquake, and water damage).

AMBIGUITIES — Anything doubtful, uncertain or capable of being misunderstood in an insurance contract. Ambiguities are usually construed against the insurer.

AMERICAN AGENCY SYSTEM — The contracting of insurance companies with agents who are independent contractors to effect property-liability insurance, to issue policies, to own the EXPIRATION records thereof, and in general to represent the companies in their communities. Agents may represent more than one company. The system has reached its highest development in the United States, hence "American" Agency System. See INDEPENDENT AGENT, DIRECT WRITER, and EXPIRATION.

AMERICAN ARBITRATION ASSOCIATION — An organization sponsoring voluntary arbitration for labor-management and commercial and international trade disputes. Specifically has established an Accident Claims Tribunal to service arbitration proceedings under the family protection coverage of automobile liability policies, which name the Association as administrator of arbitration. Headquarters in New York.

AMERICAN ASSOCIATION OF INSURANCE SERVICES — The rating bureau for inland marine, aircraft hull, and package insurance fields for insurers choosing to participate. Formerly Transportation Insurance Rating Bureau. Also rates homeowners policies and the inland portion of the comprehensive dwelling policy. Headquarters, Chicago.

AMERICAN ASSOCIATION OF MANAGING GENERAL AGENTS (AAMGA) — A trade association of independent insurance general agents serving the interests of insurance companies and local agents. Provides markets for all types of insurance with emphasis on surplus and specialty lines. Established in 1926. Headquarters, Washington, D.C.

AMERICAN BUREAU OF SHIPPING — A technical society, sponsored by shipowners, which sets minimum standards for ship design, materials and construction. Provides periodic surveys of ship and machinery to maintain adequate standards, and publishes American Bureau of Record listing vessels "classed." This record provides detailed information: type, size, construction material, machinery, fuel used, and date and type of last survey. Headquarters, New York, but the Bureau has correspondents in principal seaports.

AMERICAN CARGO WAR RISK REINSURANCE EXCHANGE — An association of companies writing ocean marine business, formed for the purpose of reinsuring war risks on ocean cargoes. The reinsurance facilities established by this organization permitted member companies to provide automatic cargo coverage to importers and exporters even during the worst part of World War II. Headquarters in New York.

AMERICAN COLLEGE, THE (formerly The American College of Life Underwriters) — Founded in 1927, The American College is a private, nonprofit educational institution for the advancement of learning and professionalism in life insurance and related financial sciences. Those properly qualified persons who successfully pass the examinations this college prepares are awarded the designation, "Chartered Life Underwriter" (CLU), or the graduate degree of "Master of Science in Financial Services." Headquarters, Bryn Mawr, Pennsylvania.

AMERICAN COUNCIL OF LIFE INSURANCE — A public relations organization representing legal reserve life insurance in legislative and administrative matters at federal, state, and municipal levels of government. Conducts economic and social research programs, compiles statistics, and publishes pamphlets and consumer booklets. Headquarters, Washington, D.C.

AMERICAN FOREIGN INSURANCE ASSOCIATION (AFIA) — A group of American stock insurance companies writing insurance in countries other than the United States on a joint or cooperative basis. Headquarters, New York.

AMERICAN HULL INSURANCE SYNDICATE — This is an association of insurance companies writing hull, war risk and builders risk coverage on the larger commercial vessels. Formed to provide a ready and sufficient market for American and foreign ships, management issues its own policy and settles losses on behalf of subscriber companies. Headquarters, New York.

AMERICAN INSTITUTE FOR PROPERTY AND LIABILITY UNDERWRITERS, INC. — An insurance educational organization which establishes insurance educational standards and fosters educational work. Those properly qualified persons who successfully pass the examinations this body prepares are awarded the designation "Chartered Property and Casualty Underwriter" (CPCU). Headquarters, Malvern, Pennsylvania.

AMERICAN INSTITUTE OF MARINE UNDERWRITERS — An association of marine insurance writing companies which provides a meeting place for discussion of common problems. Operates many technical committees which produce marine forms and clauses and other important information for marine underwriters. Headquarters, New York.

AMERICAN INSURANCE ASSOCIATION (AIA) — A trade association of primarily stock property and casualty insurers that performs numerous functions: fire and accident prevention, reviews of insurance legislation, research, building and fire department standards, arson and fraudulent claims investigations, etc. Headquarters, New York.

AMERICAN INTERNATIONAL UNDERWRITERS CORPORATION (AIU) — Acting as foreign manager for a group of American stock insurance companies, this corporation underwrites all classes of insurance on properties and risks outside the United States and Canada. Headquarters, New York.

AMERICAN LLOYDS — Associations of individual underwriters operating in the United States. No connection with Lloyd's of London and in no way a similar organization. Only permitted to operate in a limited number of states.

AMERICAN MUTUAL INSURANCE ALLIANCE — See ALLIANCE OF AMERICAN INSURERS.

AMERICAN NUCLEAR INSURERS — A syndicate of stock property and casualty companies formed to write material damage and liability insurance on industry-operated nuclear reactors and related operations. Headquarters, Farmington, Connecticut. Formerly known as Nuclear Energy Liability-Property Insurance Association (NEL-PIA).

AMERICAN RISK AND INSURANCE ASSOCIATION — An association of those engaged in teaching insurance and risk management in colleges and universities. Lay persons interested in the Association's objectives of scholarly research in the fields of risk and insurance are also eligible for membership. Publishes a quarterly scholarly journal, *The Journal of Risk and Insurance*. Formerly the American Association of University Teachers of Insurance. Headquarters, Athens, Georgia.

AMERICAN SOCIETY OF INSURANCE MANAGEMENT INC. (ASIM) — See RISK AND INSURANCE MANAGEMENT SOCIETY, INC. (RIMS).

AMERICAN TRIAL LAWYERS ASSOCIATION (ATLA) — See ASSOCIATION OF TRIAL LAWYERS OF AMERICA (ATLA).

13

AMORTIZATION — Periodical write-down of premium paid on purchase of a bond or write-up of discount received on purchase of a bond so as to reach par value at maturity date.

AMORTIZED VALUE — The current appraised worth of any bond not yet matured and which was either bought at a discount (less than its face value) or at a premium (more than its face value). For example, a bond bought today at $1,050 to mature in 10 years would have an amortized value one year hence of $1,045, two years hence of $1,040, etc.

AMOUNT OF INSURANCE — A limit of payment a company can be liable for under a policy.

AMOUNT SUBJECT — See MAXIMUM POSSIBLE LOSS.

ANALYTIC SYSTEM FOR THE MEASUREMENT OF RELATIVE FIRE HAZARDS — See DEAN SCHEDULE.

ANNUAL RENEWAL AGREEMENT — Certain policy forms contain a clause whereby the company agrees to renew the policy for a certain number of times at some specified rate.

ANNUAL STATEMENT — A summary of an insurance company's operations for the year, and a balance sheet at the end of the year, supported by detailed exhibits and schedules, and filed with the insurance department of each state wherein the company is licensed to conduct an insurance business. Details and the precise form of the ANNUAL STATEMENT are prescribed by the NAIC. Also known as Convention Blank.

ANNUALIZATION — The term which applies to the provision whereby a policy issued for a period of more than one year is subject to the payment of annual premiums, often with the proviso that the annual payment is made at the premium rate prevailing at the anniversary date. Applicable to property insurance policies.

ANTITRUST LAWS — Anti-compact laws which forbid companies from agreeing on prices, products, and other business conditions to the detriment of competition, except under conditions stated in the laws.

ANTI-DISCRIMINATORY LAWS — Laws which prohibit a company from playing favorites. Every rate must be fair and representative of the risk and its hazard. See UNFAIR DISCRIMINATION.

APARTMENT PACKAGE POLICY — A package policy forming part of the SPECIAL MULTI-PERIL POLICY program combining the various coverages applicable to the ownership and operation of an apartment house. Basically it covers fire, allied lines, and liability; and it can be extended for other coverages, such as boiler and machinery, glass, fidelity, etc.

14

APPLICATION — In all types of insurance requiring it, a written statement by a prospective policyholder which gives the information the company relies upon when issuing the insurance. In England this is called a proposal.

APPOINTMENT — The act by a company of authorizing an agent to act for it.

APPORTIONMENT — The process by which one determines how much each policy on a risk must pay when there is more than one policy involved in a loss.

APPRAISAL — Valuation of property.

APPRAISAL CLAUSE — The clause in a policy which sets forth the conditions under which a disputed loss is decided by appraisers. See ARBITRATION CLAUSE.

APPRAISER — 1) A person who determines the value of property. 2) A party who determines the amount of a disputed loss.

APPRECIATION — The amount by which property has increased in value. See DEPRECIATION.

APPROVED — A term rather loosely used to mean something which meets the standards set up by insurers, e.g., approved roof or approved cargo.

APPROVED ROOF — Usually a roof made of fire-resistive material as distinguished from wood.

ARBITRATION CLAUSE — Language in most policies of insurance providing that, in the event the company and the claimant are unable to agree on the amount due after loss, the matter shall be submitted to disinterested parties for solution. One party is appointed by the insured, one by the company, and the two appointed arbitrators then pick a third, the "umpire."

ARBITRATOR — One chosen to decide disputes out of court.

ARCHITECTS AND ENGINEERS PROFESSIONAL LIABILITY INSURANCE — Protects architects and engineers against claims arising out of their professional services caused by error, omission, or negligent acts.

ARSON — The intentional burning of property.

A. S. — An indication on a diagram that the risk is protected by automatic sprinklers.

ASSAILING THIEVES — A term used in ocean marine policies to indicate insurance against theft by physical force from persons other than ship's officers or crew.

15

ASSESSABLE INSURANCE — A type of insurance which may require the policyholder to contribute in the event the insurer becomes unable to pay its losses. Confined to certain mutual companies. See NONASSESSABLE.

ASSESSMENT — The charge levied by an insurer writing an assessable policy (as sold by some mutual insurers), in addition to the policy premium, in the event the insurer becomes unable to pay its total losses.

ASSETS — All the property and resources of a business. See ADMITTED ASSETS.

ASSIGNED RISK PLAN — See AUTOMOBILE INSURANCE PLAN.

ASSIGNMENT — Transferring property rights to another. Insurance policies may thus be assigned or transferred to another, but usually this requires the consent of the insurer.

ASSOCIATED AVIATION UNDERWRITERS (AAU) — A multi-company aviation pool writing a substantial volume of most types of aviation business, both domestic and international. Founded in 1929. Headquarters, New York.

ASSOCIATION OF AVERAGE ADJUSTERS — Professional organization of persons involved in the adjustment of maritime losses with a specific emphasis on the ancient concept of general average (a loss common to all interests in the voyage). Headquarters, New York.

ASSOCIATION OF TRIAL LAWYERS OF AMERICA (ATLA) — Successor to National Association of Claimants Compensation Attorneys (NACCA). A countrywide association of plaintiffs' lawyers mainly engaged in the field of personal injury law which, by meetings, lectures, seminars and publications exchanges ideas and develops techniques for the successful prosecution of their cases and the award of higher court judgments. Name changed from American Trial Lawyers Association (1973). Headquarters, Cambridge, Mass.

ASSUME — To accept (by an underwriter or other person authorized to act) all or part of a risk or an exposure, at which time insurance "attaches." See ACCEPT.

ASSUME LIABILITY — Contractual liability which arises from agreement between people as opposed to liability which arises from common or statute law.

ASSUMPTION ENDORSEMENT — See CUT-THROUGH ENDORSEMENT.

ASSURANCE — Same as "insurance" but used more in England and more often restricted to "life assurance" (insurance). See INSURANCE.

16

ASSURED — The person or party protected by a policy of insurance. Same as insured. See POLICYHOLDER.

ATTACH — The commencement of insurance coverage in a policy (on its effective date or when its term starts).

ATTESTATION CLAUSE — The clause in a policy which identifies the required signature of an officer of the insurer authorizing the coverage.

ATTORNEY-IN-FACT — One who has been given specific authority to act for another in certain clearly defined matters. Often used in insurance to refer to the person or entity operating a "reciprocal exchange" or "inter-insurance exchange."

ATTRACTIVE NUISANCE — A condition which, although normally harmless, may nevertheless attract those (usually children) who do not understand its uses and may cause injury. Although it may be proper to maintain such condition, the owner is nevertheless required to take such means as may be necessary to prevent its causing injury to innocent people, e.g., an empty swimming pool, an unattended tractor, or an upended ladder.

AUDIT — Verification of books or accounts to determine their accuracy. Certain policies written on a reporting or adjustable form give the insurer the privilege of auditing the policyholder's records to verify the accuracy of the premiums paid.

AUDIT BUREAU — An office which checks rates and forms of issued policies for accuracy of rates and rules. Sometimes called STAMPING BUREAU because the daily report is stamped with a rubber stamp if correctly prepared.

AUDITOR — One who checks the accuracy of figures: the company's or those of its policyholders who are insured by policies permitting or calling for audits. Payroll auditors in workers compensation insurance are a good example.

AUTHORIZATION — A statement, written or oral, made by an underwriter to a producer, expressing the underwriter's ability, willingness, and readiness to insure a certain risk for a certain amount on certain terms.

AUTHORIZED COMPANY — An insurer licensed by the state insurance department to write certain types of insurance in that state. A synonym for licensed or admitted company.

AUTOMATIC COVER — Policy protection applied simultaneously with the acquisition of new property similar to that already covered by the policy. Certain policies provide that they will assume liability for property other than that covered at the commencement of the contract if and when the policyholder acquires ownership or in the event of some similar happening which the policy describes.

AUTOMATIC REINSTATEMENT — After a loss has been paid or the damaged property restored, most policies provide the amount of insurance will automatically return to its original amount. Some policies are reduced by the amount of loss paid, but can be reinstated for additional premium.

AUTOMATIC SPRINKLERS — A system to protect property from severe damage by fire in which water is piped to devices called sprinkler heads, which melt with heat and release water to extinguish a fire. Extensively used to protect valuable properties, and property so protected normally is charged a lower fire insurance rate than property not so protected.

AUTOMATIC TREATY — A reinsurance agreement between re-insured and reinsurer (usually for pro rata reinsurance, and usually for one year or longer), whereby the ceding company is obligated to cede certain risks as provided in the agreement and the reinsurer is obligated to accept.

AUTOMOBILE DEATH AND DISABILITY COVERAGE — A form of accident insurance coverage available under a private passenger Automobile Liability policy whereby the insurer pays a principal sum for accidental death, stated benefits for specific injuries (such as loss of limbs, fractures, etc.), and weekly indemnity for total disability. Covers accidents while traveling in an automobile, including getting in and out—or by being struck by an automobile. An extra premium is charged for this coverage which is available to the policyholder, a spouse, or any other named person.

AUTOMOBILE FLEET — A group of automobiles, used commercially and owned or leased by the insured, which may get special rate treatment.

AUTOMOBILE INSURANCE — Any kind of insurance pertaining to the ownership, maintenance, or use of automobiles.

AUTOMOBILE INSURANCE PLAN — An association of insurers in a given state in which automobile risks unable to get insurance in the voluntary market are shared among subscribing insurers in proportion to the amount of automobile liability insurance each insurer writes in that state. All companies writing this class are required to participate in this activity, currently administered by the National Industry Committee on Automobile Insurance Plans, with headquarters in New York. Long identified as "assigned risk plans," such plans sometimes take the form of joint underwriting associations.

AUTOMOBILE LIABILITY EXCESS POLICY — Provides excess limits for bodily injury and property damage liability for persons unable to secure more than minimum limits under their basic

18

automobile liability insurance. Mostly purchased by assigned risk plan policyholders, the excess insurance always stipulates that the primary policy must be kept in force.

AUTOMOBILE LIABILITY INSURANCE — Protection for loss incurred through legal liability for bodily injury and damage to property of others caused by accidents arising out of ownership, maintenance, or use of an automobile.

AUTOMOBILE MEDICAL PAYMENTS INSURANCE — An optional coverage under an automobile liability policy which pays the medical expenses of the policyholder and any of the passengers injured by the insured automobile, irrespective of who was responsible for the accident. This was originally called "basic medical payments." In addition, it pays the medical expenses of the policyholder and members of the immediate family injured while passengers in any other automobile or struck by an automobile. In some no-fault states, medical payments insurance has been replaced by personal injury protection (PIP); in other states, it may supplement no-fault insurance. See PERSONAL INJURY PROTECTION.

AUTOMOBILE PHYSICAL DAMAGE INSURANCE — Material damage insurance covering loss or damage to the policyholder's automobile. See COMBINATION AUTOMOBILE POLICY.

AUXILIARY YACHT — A pleasure boat propelled by both sail and power.

AVERAGE — 1) The ocean marine underwriter's term for loss. 2) Derived from the French *avarie*, meaning damage to ship or cargo.

AVERAGE ADJUSTER — An adjuster of marine losses, such as particular or general average.

AVERAGE CLAUSE — Language in an insurance policy which distributes the insurance among several items in proportion to their value or in a similar way. Also known as a coinsurance clause, average distribution clause, and pro rata distribution clause.

AVERAGE RATE — Since rates generally apply to individual items (i.e., a building or specific contents), when two or more such items are combined in a single "blanket" amount of insurance, the value of each item is multiplied by its own rate. The sum of the premiums thus determined is divided by the total amount of insurance on all the items to produce an average rate for all the insured property.

AVERAGE WEEKLY WAGE — 1) A calculation which reflects the average rate of remuneration of employees, used as a basis for determining benefits in workers compensation insurance. 2) A type of statistic promulgated by the U.S. Department of Labor on a national level and used for determining benefits under federal compensation acts.

AVIATION CLAUSE — Language in certain policies which describes restrictions in coverage in or on aircraft.

AVIATION INSURANCE — A broad field of protection covering both domestic and international operations of aircraft owned and used, involving hulls, liability, passenger liability, airport and hangar keepers liability.

B

BAIL BOND — A bond intended to guarantee the appearance of a person in court to answer a legal summons for personal appearance. In the event the one out on bail fails to appear, the bondsman or bonding company is required to pay the amount of the bond to the court.

BAILEE — One who has custody of the property of another. Bailees "for hire" have certain responsibilities to care for the property of others that is in their custody.

BAILEE CUSTOMERS INSURANCE — Insurance arranged by a bailee for the account of bailors or customers. An example is the insuring of furs in a storage warehouse arranged by the warehouse bailee for the benefit of the owners of the furs. Laundry bundle insurance is similar.

BAILMENT — Personal property delivered by its owner to another to be held and returned to the owner in good condition. The owner who delivers the property is called the bailor, the one who receives it the bailee.

BAILOR — A person entrusting goods to another.

BALANCE — 1) The excess on either side of a bookkeeping account. 2) The net amount due a company by an agent.

BALANCE SHEET — A statement of the assets, liabilities and owners' equity (surplus) of an enterprise. (Assets minus liabilities equals owners' equity.)

BANKER'S BLANKET BOND — A special form of bond designed to insure banks against loss from employee dishonesty, burglary, robbery, larceny, theft, forgery, misplacement and certain other perils.

BARRATRY — Wilful and illegal sinking, casting away, or damaging a ship at sea or its cargo.

BASIC LIMITS — Certain minimum amounts of liability in liability insurance (determined by custom or laws), for which "basic" premiums apply. Additional amounts of liability insurance are charged for by the addition of certain percentages of the premium charged for the minimum limits.

BASIC RATE — A fundamental rate usually applied to a whole class of policies or to similar properties in a given territory such as one state.

BENEFICIARY — The person or entity named in a life insurance policy to receive the proceeds.

BENEFITS — In life, health and accident insurance, the money payable or services rendered under the policy.

BETTERMENTS — See IMPROVEMENTS AND BETTERMENTS.

BID BOND — A bond intended to guarantee that the bidder on a construction, supply or service contract will enter into the contract if successful as a bidder. Should the bidder fail to enter the contract, the surety on the bid bond may be called upon to pay the difference between the amount of the principal's bid and the bid of the next lowest qualified bidder.

BILL OF LADING — A document, issued by the transportation carrier as receipt for the goods being shipped, which describes the voyage, vessel, date of sailing, and goods, and also states the carrier's liability, limitations and exemptions. Some bills of lading may be used as negotiable instruments. There are three types of bills of lading: under deck, on deck, and on board. See CARRIAGE OF GOODS BY SEA ACT, and HARTER ACT.

BINDER — An oral or written agreement to insure which serves as evidence of coverage prior to the issuance of a policy. See COVER NOTE.

BINDING AUTHORITY — The right one party (usually an agent) has to represent another (usually an insurer) in effecting or creating an insurance contract.

BLANKET CRIME POLICY — A blanket policy insuring against employee dishonesty, losses inside and outside the premises, losses from money orders and counterfeit paper currency, and depositor's forgery. Policy covers money, securities and other property with a single limit of insurance applying to all coverages, none of which may be eliminated. Similar to 3-D policy (COMPREHENSIVE DISHONESTY, DISAPPEARANCE, and DESTRUCTION) wherein the same coverages are afforded but on an optional basis.

21

BLANKET INSURANCE — A single amount of insurance covering several items, e.g., one amount of insurance to cover two buildings, or one building and its contents. Such policies usually require the fulfillment of certain restrictions which may not be required in "specific" or "itemized" policies, such as the use of a 90% coinsurance clause.

BLANKET POSITION BOND — A fidelity bond which insures an employer against loss from dishonest acts by employees. As the name implies, blanket coverage is granted for all employees in the regular service of the employer during the term of the bond. The bond is issued for a fixed sum and each employee is covered up to the full amount of the bond. The maximum amount payable for any one embezzlement involving more than one employee would thus be the amount of the bond multiplied by the number of employees involved. See COMMERCIAL BLANKET BOND.

BLANKET RATE — A fire insurance rate which applies to BLANKET INSURANCE.

BLOCK LIMIT — A maximum amount of insurance an insurer is willing to write within any one city block or one block of an urban area. An uncommon practice today.

BLUE CROSS PLAN — A nonprofit, tax-exempt health service prepayment organization providing coverage for health care and related services. Unlike most private insurance companies, the plans usually provide service rather than indemnity benefits, often paying hospitals on the basis of reasonable costs (by pre-arranged agreement) rather than charges. The seventy individual plans in the U.S. should be distinguished from their national association, the Blue Cross Association.

BODILY INJURY — Injury, sickness, or disease sustained by a person, including death at any time resulting therefrom.

BODILY INJURY LIABILITY INSURANCE — A form of "third-party" protection covering the insured's legal liability for bodily injury to others caused by the insured's negligence. See LIABILITY INSURANCE.

BOILER AND MACHINERY INSURANCE — Protection against loss from disruption of boilers and machinery by an insured peril: loss to the boiler and machinery itself, damage to other property, business interruption losses, or all three. Also known as Machinery Breakdown Insurance.

BOND, FIDELITY — An insurance policy which reimburses an employer for employee theft or embezzlement.

BOND, SURETY — A written agreement wherein one party, called the surety, obligates itself to a second party, called the obligee or beneficiary, to answer for the default of a third party, called the principal.

BOOK VALUE — The dollar amount of assets (bonds, stocks, real estate, etc.) shown in a company's books.

BORDERLINE RISK — An average in terms of loss potential, neither unusually good or bad.

BORDEREAU — A report by an insurance company to its reinsurer listing and summarizing certain insurance transactions affecting the reinsurance.

BOTTOMRY — In the early days of marine insurance, a ship owner would borrow money by mortgaging the ship, and the mortgage would provide that if the ship were lost, the borrower would not have to repay the loan. This was bottomry, which thus combined money lending with insurance. When cargo instead of hull was involved, it was called RESPONDENTIA.

BRANCH OFFICE — A territorial office, reporting to home or head office, supervising business in its operational area and providing agency service by a staff of special agents, underwriters, claims personnel, auditors and engineers.

BRICK BUILDING — A type of construction in which the outer walls are at least the thickness of two bricks in width. See BRICK VENEER and FRAME BUILDING.

BRICK VENEER — A building the outer walls of which are made of wood faced with a single course of brick. In other words, it is a frame building with a brick outside covering, as distinguished from a brick building in which the supporting walls are brick. See BRICK BUILDING and FRAME BUILDING.

BRIDGE POLICY — Special inland marine forms which insure bridges against many hazards.

BROAD FORM STOREKEEPERS POLICY — A package designed to provide broad crime insurance for small retail stores. It principally insures against loss of money and securities, merchandise burglary losses, and losses from employee dishonesty and forgery. A more restricted and less costly coverage, the Storekeepers' Burglary and Robbery policy, is also available for retail stores.

BROKER — A licensed, legal representative of the insured who negotiates with underwriters on behalf of the insured. Nevertheless, the broker receives a commission from the insurer (underwriter).

BROKER-AGENT — Large agents at times operate both as brokers representing the policyholder and as agents representing the company. Or they may have an office in one city which operates strictly on a brokerage basis and one in another city in which they are agents.

BROKER OF RECORD — A licensed broker who has been designated by the policyholder to represent that policyholder.

BUILDERS RISK — 1) A building or a ship in the course of construction. 2) A special form dealing with the unique loss exposure of property under construction.

BUILDING CODE — A set of laws which prescribe the standards by which buildings must be constructed in a city which has adopted the code.

BUILDING RATE — The fire insurance rate on a building as distinguished from the rate for insurance on its contents.

BULLION — Gold or silver insured for its value as metal and not for its value as coin.

BURGLAR ALARMS — Devices of various types which give warning of entry into premises by unauthorized persons. Burglary insurance premium discounts are allowed for burglar alarm systems approved by the UNDERWRITERS LABORATORIES.

BURGLARY — Theft by forceable and illegal entry, evidenced by visible signs made by tools, explosives, electricity or chemicals.

BURGLARY AND THEFT INSURANCE — Insurance against loss of property (from the various types of theft or damage) caused by burglary or theft.

BURNING RATIO — The ratio of losses suffered to the amount of insurance in effect. Thus, not a "loss ratio," which is the ratio of loss to premium. See PURE PREMIUM.

BUSINESS AUTO POLICY — Coverage designed to provide a "standard" form for insuring commercial vehicles (other than private passenger cars).

BUSINESS INTERRUPTION INSURANCE — A form of indirect damage coverage under property insurance policies which protects against loss of income. The loss is determined by calculating gross earnings and subtracting noncontinuing expenses.

"BUY-BACK" DEDUCTIBLE — A deductible which may be removed by payment of additional premium when full coverage is required.

BY ORDER OF CIVIL AUTHORITY — A directive of city officials or other civil authority that a building may be destroyed by the fire department to prevent the spread of conflagration. See CIVIL AUTHORITY CLAUSE.

C

CALENDAR YEAR EXPERIENCE — See ACCIDENT YEAR EXPERIENCE.

CAMERA FLOATER — An inland marine form designed to insure cameras and their equipment.

CANCEL — To terminate a contract. Usually applied to the termination of a policy before its natural expiration, but may be used to describe the ending of any contract during its natural life, such as an agent's contract.

CANCELLATION — The termination of a contract before its normal ending. See CANCEL.

CAPACITY — The amount of insurance (measured either by face value of policies or by premium) which an insurer is able or willing to issue as a maximum, as limited by legal restrictions, corporate restrictions, or indirect restrictions. Legal restrictions (e.g., "no policy may be issued for an amount in excess of 10% of policyholder surplus") or corporate restrictions (e.g., a board of directors resolution that "the company shall not knowingly commit itself to a policy amount in excess of $10 million") establish the maximum capacity an insurer is able to write. Indirect restrictions on the capacity an insurer is willing to write include: a) the financial strength (policyholder surplus) of the insurer, or b) the willingness of the insurer to venture a portion of its current anticipated underwriting (or overall) profit on a single policy (this willingness could also be expressed as a percent of annual premium) and the confidence felt in that anticipated result.

CAPITAL STOCK INSURANCE — Insurance business transacted by an insurer whose ownership element is divided into shares of stock represented by certificates, as opposed to a mutual insurer which does not have capital stock and whose ownership element is divided among its policyholders. While a stock insurer has both stockholders (its owners) and policyholders (its customers), a mutual insurer has only policyholders (its owners and customers). See MUTUAL INSURANCE.

25

CAPTIVE AGENT — An agent who, by contract, represents only one company and its affiliates. Sometimes called "exclusive agent."

CAPTIVE INSURANCE COMPANY — A company which is wholly-owned by another organization (generally non-insurance), the main purpose of which is to insure the risks of the parent organization.

CARGO — Goods being transported by rail, plane, truck, ship, or other conveyance, excluding the equipment needed to operate the conveyor.

CARPENTER PLAN — A form of excess of loss reinsurance in which a ceding company spreads its losses over a three-to-five-year period, first introduced in the U.S. by a broker of that name. See SPREAD LOSS REINSURANCE.

CARRIAGE OF GOODS BY SEA ACT — An international agreement subscribed to by most maritime nations and ratified by the U.S. in 1936, prescribing the format and content of uniform ocean bills of lading on goods shipped internationally.

CARRIER — 1) The insurance company which provides the protection for a particular risk. 2) A transporter of goods, a form of bailee for which insurance is provided. A common carrier is one which is available to the public for the transport of any goods. A private carrier transports only the goods of its owner.

CASH FLOW PLAN — A method of paying casualty insurance premiums in which the insured (usually a large commercial concern) pays the fixed portion (administrative expenses) of the premium in installments and the variable portion (loss payments and loss reserves) as incurred.

CASUALTY ACTUARIAL SOCIETY — An organization formed to promote actuarial and statistical knowledge applicable to casualty insurance. Following multiple line development in the insurance industry, the scope of the Society has been enlarged to include all lines of insurance other than life. Headquarters in New York. Its life and health counterpart is SOCIETY OF ACTUARIES.

CASUALTY INSURANCE — Insurance concerned with legal liability for personal injuries or damage to property of others, including many other types of insurance such as workers compensation, plate glass, burglary, boiler and machinery, aviation, etc. "Casualty" is generally accepted to cover all classes outside the definition of "property insurance," so that a property and casualty company would tend to handle all forms of insurance other than life.

CATASTROPHE — A severe loss, usually involving many risks.

CATASTROPHE (EXCESS) COVER — 1) In reinsurance, a form of excess of loss reinsurance which, subject to a specified limit, indemnifies the ceding company for the amount of loss in excess of a specified retention, with respect to an accumulation of losses resulting from a catastrophic event or series of events. The actual reinsurance document is referred to as "a catastrophe cover." 2) In primary insurance, an amount of insurance on a single risk or group of risks in excess of self-insured retentions or other primary insurance.

CATASTROPHE NUMBER — Whenever a catastrophe occurs which produces losses within a prescribed period of time in excess of a certain amount (now $1 million), the amount of such losses is recorded separately from noncatastrophe losses, is numbered by the American Insurance Association, and may be treated differently in the statistical experience records of the state used in setting rate levels.

CATASTROPHE REINSURANCE — See CATASTROPHE (EXCESS) COVER.

CEDE — To pass on to another insurer (the reinsurer) all or part of the insurance written by an insurer (the ceding insurer) with the object of reducing the possible liability of the latter.

CEDING COMPANY — An insurer which has bought reinsurance protection as distinguished from the reinsurer which has issued the reinsurance protection.

CENTRAL PROCESSING UNIT — The part of an insurer's computing system containing the circuits that calculate and perform logic decisions based on a man-made program of operating instructions.

CERTIFICATE OF INSURANCE — A short-form documentation of an insurance policy.

CESSION — 1) The unit of insurance, passed to a reinsurer by a primary company which issued a policy to the original insured. A cession may accordingly be the whole or a portion of single risks, defined policies, or defined divisions of business, all as agreed in the reinsurance contract. 2) The act of ceding where such an act is necessary to invoke the reinsurance protection.

CHARTER — To rent or lease a ship.

CHARTER PARTY — The document which outlines the agreements between a ship owner and the person or organization which chartered (or leased) a ship.

CHATTEL MORTGAGE — A mortgage, the collateral for which is personal or movable property, as distinguished from a mortgage on land or buildings.

C.I.F. (COST, INSURANCE AND FREIGHT) — A sale term indicating the purchaser is required to pay for the cost, insurance, and freight in shipping purchased goods to their indicated destination.

CIVIL AUTHORITY CLAUSE — A provision in a policy requiring the payment of the loss suffered by the policyholder if the insured property is destroyed by the city, or other civil authority, in an effort to prevent the spread of fire.

CIVIL COMMOTION — A disturbance among, or a popular uprising of, a large number of people.

CLAIM — An amount requested of an insurer, by a policyholder or a claimant, for an insured loss.

CLAIM AGENT — In marine insurance, a person authorized by a marine underwriter to survey and certify losses. Underwriters maintain claim agents in various important ports and cities throughout the world. Claim agents do not have the authority to pay losses as do SETTLING AGENTS.

CLAIM DEPARTMENT — The personnel of an insurance company dealing with losses or claims. In casualty operations it is a "claim" department, in fire operations, a "loss" department. As the property and liability business develops more on a multi-line basis, these distinctions are rapidly disappearing.

CLAIMANT — One who presents a claim, or one who has suffered a collectible loss. See PLAINTIFF.

CLAIMS-MADE — A liability insurance method covering losses from claims asserted against the insured during the policy period, regardless of whether the liability-imposing causes occurred during or prior to the policy period. (However, many underwriters may not cover liability-imposing causes occurring prior to the policy period.) The traditional "occurrence" liability insurance method, on the other hand, provides coverage for losses from liability-imposing causes which occurred during the policy period, regardless of when the claim is asserted. Once the policy period is over in a claims-made form, the approximate extent of the underwriter's liability is known. With the traditional "occurrence" liability coverage method, the underwriter may not discover the extent of liability for years to come from losses claimed to have occurred within the policy period. See LONG TAIL.

CLASS RATE — Rates are made for fire insurance or its allied lines, either specifically (a separate rate for the particular property in question) or for all risks of a given classification (e.g., to all frame dwellings).

CLASSIFICATION — The systematic arranging of properties, persons, or business operations into groups or categories according to certain criteria. The purposes of such classification in insurance are to create bases for establishing statistical experience and determining rates, and to avoid unfair discrimination. The essential concept of establishing classifications is that each risk should bear its fair share of the overall cost of expenses and losses in relation to its own relevant expenses and hazard. It is unfair discrimination to charge different rates for similar risks, and it is equally wrong to treat risks the same which have different costs and expenses. See UNFAIR DISCRIMINATION.

CLASSIFICATION SOCIETY — An organization which institutes standards for construction of large vessels, with follow-up surveys periodically or after accidents. The object of such a society is to maintain minimum standards for cargo carrying vessels to reduce hull and cargo insurance costs. The Society is supported by fees charged to shipowners for services rendered and publishes an annual register of approved vessels.

CLAUSE — Language in a policy which describes, limits, or modifies coverage granted.

CLEAR-SPACE CLAUSE — Language which requires that the property insured be separated from some other property, e.g., from stacks of lumber or from the forest.

CLIENT — The customer (person or entity) which buys insurance through an agent or other intermediary.

CLOSE OUT — To complete a binder through issuance of the corresponding policy.

CLU (CHARTERED LIFE UNDERWRITER) — The professional designation conferred by The American College (formerly The American College of Life Underwriters).

COASTAL WATERS — For the insurance of yachts and outboard motor boats, the waters of bays and inlets, as well as of the sea along the coast. Also referred to as contiguous waters.

CODE — A number assigned to represent some characteristic of a risk, e.g., its state of location, its occupancy class, or the type of policy involved.

COIL — See CONFERENCE OF INSURANCE LEGISLATORS.

COINSURANCE CLAUSE — 1) In property insurance, a clause requiring the insured to maintain insurance at least equal to stipulated percentage of value in order to collect partial losses in full. If the insurance is less than the minimum required, that proportion of the loss will be paid which the amount of insurance carried bears to the amount which should have been carried. Symbolically:

$$\frac{\text{Insurance Carried}}{\text{Insurance Required}} \times \text{Loss} = \text{Payment} \quad (\text{subject to policy limit})$$

2) In major medical insurance, the clause which specifies the percentage of a loss which the company will pay and the percentage which the insured will bear (e.g., 80-20, 75-25).

COINSURER — 1) An insured which has not carried the required amount of insurance and must bear a portion of the loss proportionate to the inadequacy. 2) In countries other than the United States, an insurer which shares a risk with one or more other insurers. 3) An insured or an insurance company which participates with an insurer in bearing losses covered by a particular policy.

COLLEGE OF INSURANCE, THE — A fully accredited collegiate institution offering an associate degree with majors in various aspects of the insurance business, a Bachelor of Business Administration degree with an insurance major, a Bachelor of Science degree in actuarial science, and a Master of Business Administration degree with an insurance major. In addition, nine professional certificates are awarded. The day program of the College is a cooperative work-study program with alternating four-month periods of school and work with a sponsoring institution. The College, which is sponsored by the Insurance Society of New York, also sponsors management seminars, seminars for insurance commissioners, technical seminars, and home study courses. Offices are in New York and Los Angeles.

COLLISION INSURANCE — Coverage for the loss resulting from the striking of another object by a moving vehicle.

COLLISION OF THE LOAD — The striking of another object by the cargo of a moving vehicle, as opposed to the vehicle itself striking the object. In insuring merchandise in transit by motor truck, many policies insure against collision damage only if the vehicle itself collides with something. This excludes collision damage if, for example, a part of the load extends beyond the limits of the truck and hits a bridge or some other object.

COMBINATION AUTOMOBILE POLICY — A policy combining the coverages afforded under automobile physical damage and automobile liability policies.

COMBINED RATIO — The addition of the ratio of losses incurred to earned premiums, and the ratio of underwriting expenses to written premiums.

COMMERCIAL BLANKET BOND — A fidelity bond which insures an employer against loss from dishonest acts committed by employees, covering all employees in the regular service of the employer during the term of the bond. The bond is issued for a fixed amount which is the maximum sum payable for any one embezzlement, whether one or more employees are involved. See BLANKET POSITION BOND.

COMMERCIAL LINES — Types of insurance written for businesses instead of individuals (for which the term PERSONAL LINES applies).

COMMERCIAL MULTIPLE PERIL — A general term, sometimes shortened to Commercial Multi-Peril, relating to that class of package policies which provides both property and liability coverage for business risks. See SPECIAL MULTI-PERIL POLICY.

COMMERCIAL PROPERTY POLICY — An all-risk, worldwide policy covering business property.

COMMISSION — The portion of the premium paid the agent or broker for having produced the business.

COMMISSIONER OF INSURANCE — The official of a state charged with the duty of enforcing its insurance laws. Also called the Superintendent of Insurance (in three states) and Director of Insurance (in eight states). The official is elected in 11 states, appointed by a governor or state agency in 38 states, and a Civil Service appointee in Colorado.

COMMITMENTS — Amounts of insurance on risks which a company has written or agreed to write.

COMMON LAW — Law based on precedents that have been made by courts throughout the year in Great Britain and the United States. This is, therefore, law that has not been enacted into statutes by law-making bodies (which make "statute" law).

COMPARATIVE NEGLIGENCE — A more modern system of allocating damages between two or more persons than the method of contributory negligence, which remains effective in many states (under which one cannot collect damages for bodily injury or property damage caused by another's negligence if one were himself in any way negligent). Under comparative negligence, the damages collectible in relation to another person are diminished in proportion to one's degree of negligence. In most instances, damages cannot be collected at all if the claimant's negligence were greater than that of the other party. Currently, in a few instances, the courts have awarded both parties damages as a percent of the total damages, depending on respective degrees of fault.

COMPENSATION INSURANCE — See WORKERS COMPENSATION INSURANCE.

COMPLETED OPERATIONS COVERAGE — Protection for a business which sells service instead of products against liability claims arising out of work completed away from the business premises. Differs from product liability coverage, which protects against product liability claims.

COMPOSITION ROOF — A roof made of asphalt shingles, asbestos shingles or tar paper roofing, or the usual forms of roofing materials. It does not refer to slate roofs, tile roofs, or metal roofs, which are not combustible, nor does it refer to wood shingle roofs, which are usually so designated.

COMPREHENSIVE AUTOMOBILE COVERAGE — "All-risk" physical damage protection for automobiles, except for loss by collision or upset (which may be added).

COMPREHENSIVE AUTOMOBILE LIABILITY POLICY — The broadest form of business coverage for claims alleging bodily injury or property damage resulting from the insured's ownership, maintenance, or use of an automobile. The premium, which is adjusted (audited) at the expiration of the policy term, is based on the insured's actual exposure during the policy term.

COMPREHENSIVE CRIME COVERAGE ENDORSEMENT — Language attached to a Special Multi-Peril policy providing optional employee dishonesty, money and securities, money orders and counterfeit paper currency and depositors forgery coverages.

COMPREHENSIVE DISHONESTY, DISAPPEARANCE AND DESTRUCTION POLICY — Commonly known as the 3-D policy, a package policy providing crime protection principally covering dishonesty, forgery, loss of money and securities, and safe deposit losses.

COMPREHENSIVE DWELLING POLICY — A package policy for dwelling risks combining fire and allied lines coverage with comprehensive personal liability and theft insurance. An alternative coverage to homeowners policies, the CDP is rapidly becoming obsolete.

COMPREHENSIVE GENERAL LIABILITY POLICY — The broadest form business policy providing premises and operations liability coverage and optional products, contractual, and independent contractors liability coverage for claims alleging bodily injury or property damage. The premium, which is adjusted (audited) at the expiration of the policy term, is based on coverages selected and the insured's actual exposures during the policy term.

COMPREHENSIVE PERSONAL LIABILITY — A form of liability insurance which reimburses the policyholder, if liable, to pay money for damage or injury caused to others. This form does not include automobile liability, but does include almost every activity of the policyholder except such as may arise from the operations of a business, hence "personal" liability. The coverage is a part of either homeowners or tenants policies and is almost obsolete as a separate policy.

COMPULSORY INSURANCE — Coverage required by certain states of certain people in certain circumstances, e.g., workers compensation and automobile liability.

CONCEALMENT — In insurance, a failure to disclose a material fact which may void an insurance policy. See MATERIAL FACT.

CONCURRENT INSURANCE — Coverage in one policy on the same property under the same conditions as another policy.

CONDITION — Something established or agreed upon to be necessary to make a policy of insurance effective. See WARRANTY.

CONDITIONAL SALES FLOATER — An inland marine policy covering property which has been sold on the installment plan. Also known as INSTALLMENT SALES FLOATER.

CONDOMINIUM — A form of real estate ownership becoming increasingly popular. It is the individual ownership of a single unit in a multiple unit building or group of buildings, together with a percentage interest in that part of the total property owned jointly by all unit owners. In an apartment building, each apartment would be a unit and the stairways, pathways and parking areas would be in common ownership. Condominium property requires special insurance treatment.

CONFERENCE OF INSURANCE LEGISLATORS (COIL) — An organization of state legislators who specialize in insurance legislation.

CONFLAGRATION — A sweeping fire which destroys many properties and usually involves large values.

CONFLAGRATION AREA — An area in which property may be consumed by a sweeping fire, or conflagration.

CONSEQUENTIAL LOSS — A reduction in value of property (not physically damaged) caused by damage to other property. Examples: food spoilage from a change in temperature due to the damage of a refrigerator by fire, while the food itself is not damaged by the fire; or the reduction in the value of suit-jackets whose trousers have been damaged.

CONSTRUCTIVE TOTAL LOSS — Damage to property which is so great that the cost of recovering and repairing the property would exceed the insured value. See ABANDONMENT.

CONTACT LENS INSURANCE — Reimburses for replacement of lost or damaged contact lenses.

CONTENTS RATE — The fire insurance rate on the contents of a building as distinguished from the rate for insurance on the building itself.

CONTINGENCY RESERVE — 1) Assets maintained by an insurance company to absorb some unexpected outgo or loss, such as the sudden fall in the value of securities owned. Companies may carry as a contingency reserve the excess between the market value of securities on the last day of the year over their NAIC required valuation. 2) A voluntary reserve not specifically assigned.

CONTINGENT BUSINESS INTERRUPTION — The insurance against loss due to interruption of business by fire or other insured PERIL occurring at the premises of another on whom the continuation of the business is dependent, such as the premises of a supplier or a large customer.

CONTINGENT COMMISSION — A profit-sharing commission, paid to an agent, which depends upon the profit the company has realized from the agency's operations. Also known as profit-sharing commission.

CONTINGENT LIABILITY — 1) A liability which may be incurred by an insured as a result of negligence on the part of independent persons engaged to perform work. The most common example is the contingent liability of a principal contractor, which may result from construction operations undertaken by subcontractors. Also applies to the liability of a principal for the acts of an agent or servant. See PROTECTIVE LIABILITY INSURANCE. 2) In property damage insurance, the possibility of financial loss to a policyholder, resulting from damage or loss to the property of another, e.g., a supplier or a customer.

CONTRACT BOND — In general terms, a surety bond guaranteeing the performance of a contract, usually associated with construction work, but possible for almost any kind of contract. Sometimes called a performance bond.

CONTRACTORS EQUIPMENT FLOATER — An inland marine form which insures the equipment, tools and materials of a contractor.

CONTRACTORS PROTECTIVE LIABILITY — See OWNERS AND CONTRACTORS PROTECTIVE LIABILITY INSURANCE.

CONTRACTUAL LIABILITY — A legal obligation voluntarily assumed under the terms of a contract, as distinguished from liability imposed by the law (legal liability).

34

CONTRIBUTION — The amount payable by each of several policies covering a loss.

CONTRIBUTION CLAUSE — The clause in a policy which describes how much its issuer must pay if there is insurance in more than one company on a given loss.

CONTRIBUTORY INSURANCE — Group insurance in which all or part of the premium is paid by the employee or group member, with any remainder being paid by the employer or union. In noncontributory insurance, the employer pays all the premium without any contributions from employees.

CONTRIBUTORY NEGLIGENCE — A common law defense in which the plaintiff must be entirely free from fault in order to recover from a negligent defendant. If the plaintiff has in any way been guilty of neglect, the plaintiff cannot recover from the defendant. This principle has been modified in some states by legislation and interpretation by the courts. See COMPARATIVE NEGLIGENCE.

CONTRIBUTORY VALUE CLAUSE — Used in ocean marine hull, cargo, and freight policies, setting forth the insured's responsibilities and the underwriter's obligations, with respect to the insured's interest, when involved in a general average and/or an act of salvage. The insured can be a coinsurer if the insured's interest is underinsured. See GENERAL AVERAGE.

CONVENTION BLANK — Another name for ANNUAL STATEMENT, a form of financial report prescribed by the NAIC.

CONVERSION — The wrongful exercise of ownership rights over another's personal property, whether by taking, withholding or misusing.

CONVERTIBLE COLLISION — A form of full coverage collision insurance for automobiles in which 50% of the full coverage premium is charged as an initial premium, the remaining 50% being payable only if the policyholder makes a claim during the policy period. Thus, the effect is that the policyholder is not likely to make a claim unless the amount of the loss exceeds the initial premium, in which case the premium payable is changed (or converted) from 50% of the full cover rate to 100%. Becoming obsolete.

COORDINATION OF BENEFITS — In health insurance, policy provisions used by insurers to avoid duplicate payment for losses insured under more than one insurance policy (e.g., automobile or health) by making one of the insurers the primary payer, assuring that no more than 100% of the costs are covered and preventing the claimant from making a profit.

COSURETY — One of several who participate in underwriting a surety bond.

COUNTERSIGNATURE — 1) An additional signature placed on a policy by an authorized person at the time it is issued, supplementing any other signature appearing on the printed form used for the policy. 2) When used to describe a countersignature law, the signature which must be obtained from an authorized person (usually a licensed agent or broker in a state having such a law) on a policy covering property in that state, but written by a party outside the state.

COUNTRY DAMAGE — In marine cargo insurance, damage to baled cotton caused from poor methods of baling, handling, or storing which discolor and strain the cotton.

COVER — 1) To protect with insurance. 2) The insurance itself. Same as coverage.

COVER NOTE — 1) A document issued by an agent or broker which tells the insured that the agent or broker has effected the insurance described therein. Since there are often delays in issuing formal policies, a cover note gives the insured a description of what insurance the agent or broker has put into effect. A cover note is similar to a binder although a binder usually refers to a document given by a company to an agent instead of one given by the agent to a customer. 2) Used by surplus lines brokers to evidence coverage placed with nonadmitted companies. See BINDER.

COVERAGE — The extent of insurance protection afforded by a policy of insurance.

CPCU (CHARTERED PROPERTY CASUALTY UNDER-WRITER) — The professional designation conferred by the American Institute for Property and Liability Underwriters.

CREDIBILITY — The measure of credence or belief which is attached to a particular body of statistical experience for ratemaking purposes. Generally, as the body of experience increases in volume, the corresponding credibility also increases. This term would frequently be defined in terms of specific mathematical formulas.

CREDIT CARD INSURANCE — Covers against losses stemming from the misuse of lost or misappropriated credit cards. Usually written for individuals as an endorsement to the homeowners policy, but is also offered to business corporations as a separate contract or as part of forgery of comprehensive crime policies.

CREDIT INSURANCE — 1) A form of life and health insurance protecting the lender against loss from death or disability of the borrower, often written as group insurance. The coverage can be written to protect the interest of the creditor only (single interest), or the interests of both creditor and debtor (dual interest). See SINGLE INTEREST COVER and MARGIN ACCOUNT INSURANCE. 2) Protection against loss caused by the insolvency of a firm's customers in excess of its normal credit losses; written by a few specialty casualty insurers.

CREDIT REPORT — A report on an individual's personal characteristics, credit standing, habits, and similar facts which might influence the decision to insure that individual. See INSPECTION.

CROP DUSTING AND SPRAYING LIABILITY INSURANCE — Protection against claims alleging bodily injury or property damage arising from the normal business operations of crop dusters.

CROP-HAIL INSURANCE — Insurance against hail damage to growing crops. Although hail is the basic peril in these policies, cover is often granted for crop damage resulting from additional perils such as fire, windstorm, lightning, drought, frost, excessive heat, snow, sleet, etc.

CROP-HAIL INSURANCE ACTUARIAL ASSOCIATION — Rating organization, statistical and research association for crop-hail insurance and rain insurance on public events, business ventures and private proceedings. Headquarters, Chicago.

CROP INSURANCE — See CROP-HAIL INSURANCE.

CUMULATIVE LIABILITY — Relates to fidelity bonds where a substantial claim could be made under a cancelled bond containing a DISCOVERY PERIOD and also under another bond replacing it, since defalcations of dishonest employees often are spread over lengthy periods. To avoid this cumulative liability which could expose a surety company to a loss totalling the sum of two bonds, a clause—the SUPERSEDED SURETYSHIP RIDER—is used, which picks up any liability under the prior bond and bars possibility of an accumulation of liability between the two bonds if issued by the same company.

CURTAIN WALL — Many buildings built of steel frames or concrete have walls which support no load, but merely serve to protect from the weather. Such walls are "curtain walls." Modern fire-resistive construction usually uses wall structure of this kind.

CUT-THROUGH ENDORSEMENT — An addition to an insurance policy between an insurance company and a policyholder which requires that, in the event of the company's insolvency, any part of a loss covered by reinsurance be paid directly to the policyholder by the reinsurer. The cut-through endorsement is so named because it provides that the reinsurance claim payment "cuts through" the usual route of payment from reinsured company-to-policyholder and then reinsurer-to-reinsured company, substituting instead the payment route of reinsurer-to-policyholder. The effect is to revise the route of payment only, and there is no intended increased risk to the reinsurer. Similar to the guarantee endorsement, the cut-through endorsement is also known as an Assumption Endorsement.

D

DAILY REPORT — A copy of a policy, used as the agent's or the company's record.

DATA PROCESSING EQUIPMENT INSURANCE — "All-risk" protection on equipment, software, extra expenses incurred due to failure of such equipment caused by an insured loss, and loss of earnings. Also known as an "EDP" policy. May be extended to cover liability claims alleging errors and omissions by data processing companies (this coverage is known as Data Processors E & O Insurance).

DEAN SCHEDULE — A method of rating fire insurance risks developed by A. F. Dean (Chicago, 1901). Geographically, much of the country is rated under this schedule. Known as the "Analytic System for the Measurement of Relative Fire Hazards," Dean described a standard unoccupied risk for which a base rate was named depending on overall territorial factors. Each individual hazard or factor (construction, area, damageability, occupancy, exposure, etc.) that appeared in the risk added or subtracted a percentage of the base rate to produce the specific rate. A successful, logical method which has contributed much to insurance thinking and practice.

DEBIT — 1) The amount of industrial insurance premium (usually for life insurance) due from and collectible by a DEBIT AGENT. 2) The territory assigned the DEBIT AGENT by the industrial life insurer.

DEBIT AGENT — The person who collects industrial insurance premiums (usually for life insurance) weekly or monthly from policyholders by personal contact.

DECLARATION — A statement made to the company or to its agents by a policyholder, upon which the company may rely in undertaking the insurance.

DEDUCTIBLE — In a policy providing a deductible clause, the amount which must first be subtracted from the total damage incurred before determining the insurance company's liability. Of several types used, the *straight* deductible establishes the insurer's liability above the deductible but not below it; the *franchise* deductible establishes the insurer's liability for the entire amount of damage once the deductible amount is exceeded in a loss; and the *disappearing* deductible establishes the insurer's liability for an increasing proportion of the loss, as the total damage rises above the deductible, until the deductible finally "disappears." Then the insurer is liable for the entire amount. The deductible may be in the form of an amount of dollars, a percent of the loss, a percent of the value of the insured property, or a period of time, as in health insurance (see WAITING PERIOD and ELIMINATION PERIOD).

DEFALCATION — Embezzlement as used in fidelity bonds.

DEFENSE RESEARCH INSTITUTE, INC. (DRI) — A nonprofit organization of defense lawyers engaged in personal injury litigation, formed principally to increase the skills of legal defense. Headquarters, Milwaukee.

DEFERRED PREMIUM PAYMENT PLAN — Provides for the payment of premium in installments. An initial installment is due upon attachment of liability with additional installments payable at monthly, bi-monthly or quarterly periods. The premiums due are usually in excess of the net premium earned on a short-rate basis. See CASH FLOW PLAN.

DEMOLITION INSURANCE — Insurance against the cost of removing the ruins of a building partially destroyed by an insured peril, when required by some city ordinances.

DEPOSIT PREMIUM — A tentative charge made at the beginning of certain policies, to be adjusted when the actual earned charge has been later determined. Also known as INITIAL PREMIUM.

DEPOSITORS FORGERY BOND — A bond whereby a person or corporation can insure against losses by reason of forgery or alteration of outgoing negotiable instruments only, i.e., instruments drawn against the insured's account.

DEPRECIATION — The reduction in value of tangible property caused by physical deterioration or obsolescence.

DEPRECIATION INSURANCE — Insurance which pays the difference between the depreciated value of property at the time it is damaged or destroyed by a peril insured against, and the cost of replacing it with new property of similar kind and quality. See INFLATION GUARD ENDORSEMENT.

DEVIATION — 1) A rate filing which departs from the filing made by a rating bureau. Under all-industry *prior approval* rating laws (and some earlier laws), insurers who were members of and subscribers to rating bureaus (for the class of insurance involved) were required to use the rate filed by the bureau—unless the insurers "deviated" by making a filing with an insurance department and relating their variation to the bureau filing. Deviated filings should be distinguished from independent filings where an insurer withdraws from its affiliation with the bureau for the area of the filing and files directly with the insurance department separate and apart from the bureau filing. Deviations are no longer necessary in over half the states with *open competition* type rating laws, under which an insurer has no legal obligation to adhere to the filing and may make indepentent filings while remaining a member or subscriber. 2) In marine insurance, the route taken by a vessel going to some other port or taking some other course than that described in the policy of marine insurance, contract of carriage, or bill of lading.

D.H. — On a fire insurance diagram, this designates a double hydrant for the attachment of fire hose.

DIFFERENCE IN CONDITIONS INSURANCE (DIC COVERAGE) — A policy insuring "all risks" of physical loss or damage, excluding fire and extended coverage perils. Such unnamed losses would include collapse, water damage, theft, and (optionally) flood and earthquake.

DIRECT BILLING — A system for the collection of premiums, whereby the insurance company sends a notice to the insured for the premium in lieu of the conventional collection of premiums by the agent. The company sends a statement to the agent—usually monthly—recording the premiums collected direct, and credits the agent with commission due on those items.

DIRECT DAMAGE — Loss caused from a peril which proceeds straight forward (without interruption in time or deviation in space) from its source to the damaged property.

DIRECT LOSS — See DIRECT DAMAGE.

DIRECT WRITER — A company which sells insurance to the public either through employees licensed as agents or through licensed agents, compensated on a commission basis, who represent only one company; but not through independent agents representing more than one company.

DIRECT WRITTEN PREMIUM — The policy premium, adjusted by additional or return premiums, but excluding any reinsurance premiums.

DIRECTOR OF INSURANCE — See COMMISSIONER OF INSURANCE.

DIRECTORS AND OFFICERS LIABILITY INSURANCE — Protects officers and directors of a corporation against damages from claims resulting from negligent or wrongful acts in the course of their duties. Also covers the corporation (and even the officers and directors in some cases) for expenses incurred in defending lawsuits arising from alleged wrongful acts of officers or directors. These policies always require the insured to retain part of the risk uninsured.

DISABILITY — Inability to work due to personal injury or illness. Each policy may contain its own modified definition.

DISABILITY INCOME INSURANCE — A form of coverage which provides benefits to employees disabled by sickness or accident not related to employment. An extension of workers compensation acts in New York, New Jersey, California, Hawaii, Puerto Rico and Rhode Island.

DISAPPEARING DEDUCTIBLE — A disappearing deductible is a dollar amount deducted from the amount of loss which is reduced as the size of losses increase, finally disappearing entirely (for a "large" loss) to provide full coverage when a loss reaches a certain specified figure. Deductible amounts vary from $500 to $5,000, and the limit at which the deductible disappears is usually between $5,000 and $25,000. Disappearing deductible plans are principally associated with fire policies, which thus qualify for reduced rates.

DISAPPEARING DEFICIT — Elimination of a deficit (loss) year (should one occur) from the computation of contingent commission in exchange for an annual charge in the contingent commission statement, such charge being a percentage of earned premiums.

DISBURSEMENTS — Prior to the sailing of a vessel, it is necessary to spend money for supplies, labor and other things which will be totally lost if the vessel does not complete its voyage. Insurance on "disbursements" reimburses the owner for these expenses in case the ship becomes a total loss before reaching its destination.

DISCOVERY PERIOD — A period of time, after cancellation of an insurance contract or bond, during which the insured can discover whether there would have been a recoverable loss if the contract had remained in force. The period varies considerably, and in the case of certain bonds could be indefinite by statutory requirements.

DISCRIMINATION — The exercise of choices in selecting risks, as an essential function of any insurance system, in matching individual risks with the rates representing their chances of loss or their expenses. Often used erroneously to imply unfair discrimination, which is illegal. See CLASSIFICATION and UNFAIR DISCRIMINATION.

41

DISMEMBERMENT — Loss of, and sometimes loss of use of, specified members of the body.

DISTRIBUTION CLAUSE — See PRO RATA DISTRIBUTION CLAUSE.

DIVERSIFICATION — The practice of insurance companies to spread their risks geographically, by type of insured and by peril, in order to minimize the catastrophe potential.

DIVIDEND — An amount of money paid to the policyholders of a mutual insurer because of their ownership interest. A stock corporation may also pay a dividend to its policyholders if it writes participating insurance. In either event, the amount is payable on the basis of certain savings in losses or expenses realized by the insurer on that participating class of business. See PARTICIPATING INSURANCE.

DIVISION WALL — A wall which effectively separates a building into two separate fire areas. Must meet certain standards to qualify in the making of fire insurance rates.

DOMESTIC COMPANY — An insurance company incorporated or organized under state law is a domestic insurer in that particular state. See ALIEN COMPANY and FOREIGN COMPANY.

DOMICILIARY STATE OR STATE OF DOMICILE — The state in which an insurer is incorporated. In the case of an insurer incorporated in a foreign country, the state which such insurer, "desiring to be an authorized insurer in the U.S.," has designated as its state of entry.

DOUBLE INDEMNITY — Twice the life insurance benefit, payable if death is caused by accident. Multiple indemnity is often available beyond that of double indemnity for death due to certain accidents.

DRAFT — A substitute for a check, used by many insurance companies to pay claims. A draft is payable through a named bank, which collects the amount of the draft from the issuing insurance company and then gives credit to the claimant payee's local bank.

DRAM SHOP LIABILITY INSURANCE — A form of liquor liability coverage where the basis for legal liability is a dram shop, liquor control, or alcoholic beverage law. The laws vary, but most provide that the owner of an establishment which serves alcoholic beverages is liable for injury or damage caused by an intoxicated person if it can be established that the liquor licensee caused or contributed to the intoxication of the person.

DRIVE-IN CLAIMS SERVICE — A system employed by some automobile insurers whereby vehicles with minor insured damage can be driven to the company's local "drive-in" claims office for inspection and immediate settlement of the damage claim.

DRIVE-OTHER-CAR COVERAGE — A provision in an automobile policy designed to protect the policyholder (and insureds other than the policyholder) when driving cars other than the one described in the policy.

DRIVER TRAINING CREDIT — To encourage driver education courses at schools and colleges, many insurers grant lower rates to applicants for private passenger automobile insurance who have successfully completed an approved training program.

DRY VALVE — A device in automatic sprinklers which uses air pressure to prevent water from entering the pipes in a sprinkler system until released by the opening of a sprinkler head. The object of such a dry valve is to prevent freezing of water-filled pipes and consequent bursting.

DWELLING — A house in which people live, as distinguished from a store, a factory or any other building.

E

EARLY WARNING SYSTEM — See NAIC INSURANCE REGULATORY INFORMATION SYSTEM.

EARNED PREMIUM — The portion of the policy premium allocable to the expired portion of the policy term.

EARTHQUAKE — Vibrations of the earth's crust caused by pressures from within the earth.

EARTHQUAKE INSURANCE — Insurance against damage by earthquakes and earth movement. Written most frequently on the Pacific Coast.

EDP INSURANCE — See DATA PROCESSING EQUIPMENT INSURANCE.

EFFECTIVE DATE — The day upon which a policy first becomes eligible to pay covered losses.

EFFECTS — Personal property, goods, chattels, clothes and documents.

ELECTRICAL EXEMPTION CLAUSE — A clause in a policy which provides that damage to electrical machinery by electrical current is limited to such damage as is followed by fire damage. There are several different clauses of this nature used in different circumstances.

ELIMINATION PERIOD — In health insurance, an amount of time after the occurrence of a disability during which no indemnities are payable, as provided in the policy. An elimination period can apply to accident, sickness, or to both. Commonly referred to as the WAITING PERIOD. Also used in boiler and machinery business interruption insurance.

EMBEZZLEMENT — Fraud in using money for yourself that has been entrusted by another. A similar term, CONVERSION, applies to property instead of money.

EMPLOYER'S LIABILITY INSURANCE — Coverage against the common law liability of an employer for injuries sustained by employees, as distinguished from liability imposed by a workers compensation law.

ENDORSEMENT — A document with language attached to and becoming part of a basic policy for the purpose of amplifying or modifying it, either at its inception or during its term. Any such modification can only become effective with the agreement of the insured, unless clearly made solely for the benefit of the insured.

ENGINEER — An individual in the insurance business who specializes in loss or accident prevention work and also develops rating and underwriting information.

ENGINEERS PROFESSIONAL LIABILITY POLICY — See ARCHITECTS AND ENGINEERS PROFESSIONAL LIABILITY POLICY.

ENTITLEMENT, PSYCHOLOGY OF — A concept or societal phenomenon expressing the expectation of people that their desires and wants are their legitimate needs which society can and must fulfill. The concept affects insurance when the law expands to permit increasingly more plaintiffs to recover from insurers in cases where questionable coverage exists (e.g., when courts appear eager to find that insurance coverage exists if there is any indication that the insured expected such coverage to exist, or when jury awards increase beyond economic justification).

EQUIPMENT — Personal property of a business which is not inventory or supplies; machinery and vehicles may be considered to be "equipment" for insurance purposes.

EQUIPMENT FLOATER INSURANCE — A form of inland marine insurance, often on an all-risks basis, covering various kinds of equipment. See CONTRACTORS EQUIPMENT FLOATER.

EQUITY IN UNEARNED PREMIUM RESERVE — An overstatement in the amount shown for this liability in the ANNUAL STATEMENT of an insurer. The overstatement is approximately 20-40% of an insurer's unearned premium reserve and is caused by statutory accounting requirements: 1) that initial expenses must be recorded immediately and cannot be deferred to track with premiums as they are earned and taken into revenue (as is done for expenses and income for other businesses); and 2) that the sum of all premiums representing the unexpired portions of policies on the books must be kept in the reserve. The overstatement is the amount of initial expenses recognized, which will eventually flow to the surplus account with the passage of time.

ERISA — Acronym for Employee Retirement Income Security Act of 1974, sometimes called the "pension reform act." See FIDUCIARY LIABILITY INSURANCE.

ERRORS & OMISSIONS INSURANCE — A form of Professional Liability insurance which provides coverage for mistakes made in a profession not involved with the human body (lawyers, architects, engineers) or for mistakes made in a service business (insurance, real estate, and others). See NONRECORDING CHATTEL MORTGAGE POLICY. Also a form of coverage for financial institutions protecting against loss to lending institutions which fail to effect insurance coverage. See MALPRACTICE.

ESTOPPEL — The prevention of one party from asserting rights which might otherwise have existed, by reason of that party's inequitable conduct. See WAIVER, a term sometimes used interchangeably.

EXAMINATION — An inspection of an insurance company or organization by a representative of a state insurance department to determine whether the laws of that state have been obeyed.

EXAMINATION UNDER OATH — Securing testimony after being duly sworn that such information supplied is true to the best knowledge of the testifier, under penalty of perjury or voided insurance for false statements.

EXAMINER — A representative or employee of a state insurance department delegated the task of verifying a company's records and procedures to determine that the law has been observed.

EXCESS INSURANCE — An amount of protection which bears all or a portion of a loss after the loss exceeds an agreed amount. This amount may or may not be insured elsewhere by the company issuing

45

the policy. Excess policies are not subject to the basic principle of contribution with non-excess policies, although they may contribute or share the loss with other excess policies.

EXCESS LINE — See SURPLUS LINE.

EXCESS OF LOSS RATIO REINSURANCE — See STOP LOSS REINSURANCE.

EXCESS OF LOSS REINSURANCE — A form of reinsurance whereby the reinsuring company reimburses the ceding company for the amount of loss the ceding company suffers over an agreed aggregated sum. The agreement could apply to any one loss or a number of losses arising out of any one event.

EXCHANGE — See INTERINSURANCE EXCHANGE and NEW YORK INSURANCE EXCHANGE.

EXCLUSION — 1) That which is not covered by the insurance as stated in the policy. 2) A clause in an insurance policy which specifies that which is excluded from the policy's coverage.

EXCLUSIVE AGENT — An agent who, by contract, represents only one company and its affiliates. Sometimes called a "captive agent."

EXECUTOR — A person or a corporation named in a will to administer the decedent's estate. See ADMINISTRATOR.

EXECUTRIX — A female executor.

EXEMPLARY DAMAGES — See PUNITIVE DAMAGES.

EX GRATIA PAYMENT — A payment made for which the company is not liable under the terms of its policy, usually in lieu of incurring greater legal expenses in defending a claim.

EXPEDITING CHARGES — Money spent to speed up the repair or replacement of destroyed or damaged property. Important in the adjustment of "time element" losses, such as those under business interruption forms.

EXPENSE CONSTANT — A flat premium charge made on small workers compensation policies based upon the fact that the expense factor on such risks is inadequate to cover the cost of issuing and handling the policy.

EXPENSE RATIO — Expenses incurred, expressed as a percentage of net written premiums.

EXPERIENCE — Classified statistics of claims and losses related to insurance, of outgo or of income, actual or estimated.

EXPERIENCE RATING — A form of individual risk rating which takes into consideration the loss experience of the particular risk as a

46

credit or a debit to the manual rate for the insured's classification. As the size and number of exposure units increase (e.g., a multiple location risk), more credibility is given to the insured's own experience. See MERIT RATING.

EXPIRATION — 1) The cessation of insurance when the time period for which it was written has ended. 2) The date on which insurance expires. 3) The detailed policy records of customers served which are owned by independent insurance agents. See OWNERSHIP OF EXPIRATIONS.

EXPIRATION CARD — A record of an expiration containing all important data relating to a particular insurance policy.

EXPIRATION NOTICE — A notice sent (by an insurer to an agent or broker, by an agent to a client, or by an insurer to a policyholder) to the effect that a policy is about to expire on a given date.

EXPLOSION — 1) A bursting of forces, usually from pressure within. 2) In general a rupture of a pressure vessel of some kind due to too much internal pressure, accompanied by a loud noise. Courts, however, have interpreted it in many ways.

EXPOSURE — 1) Synonymous with risk: chance of loss—by fire, radiation, accident, etc. 2) The danger of loss (particularly by fire) arising from what happens to another risk close by. 3) The sum total of values which, if damaged or destroyed, would cause loss under a policy, i.e., the value of everything a policy insures. 4) A measure of the rating units or premium basis of a risk, e.g., payroll or number of automobiles. 5) A unit of loss potential (e.g., a life, a house, an automobile, a ship, a package in shipment, an acre of growing crops, a plate glass window, a fur coat), in which case the term "exposure unit" is used.

EXTENDED COVERAGE INSURANCE — Protection against loss or damage caused by windstorm, hail, smoke, explosion, riot, civil commotion, vehicles and aircraft. Written in conjunction with a fire policy either as part of the basic contract or by endorsement.

EXTRA EXPENSE INSURANCE — Reimbursement for additional expenses incurred because of an insured loss. Written either as a separate policy or as an endorsement.

F

FACE AMOUNT — As used in life insurance, the amount stated on the first page of the policy that will be paid at maturity (upon death of the insured or expiration of the endowment period). Additional benefits may be provided by riders or dividends.

FACE VALUE — Same as FACE AMOUNT.

FACTORY INSURANCE ASSOCIATION — See INDUSTRIAL RISK INSURERS.

FACTORY MUTUALS — A group of direct-writing mutual insurance companies, independently owned and operated, which underwrite highly protected risks of substantial value on a reciprocal reinsurance basis. The central organization in New England maintains extensive fire laboratory facilities and provides its members with engineering services.

FACULTATIVE REINSURANCE — Reinsurance effected item by item and accepted or declined by the reinsuring company after scrutiny, as opposed to reinsurance effected by treaty. The word "facultative" connotes that both the primary insurer and the reinsurer have the faculty or option of accepting or rejecting the individual submission (as distinguished from the obligation to cede and accept, to which the parties agree in treaty reinsurance).

FAIR PLAN — A program to provide "Fair Access to Insurance Requirements" for property owners who experience difficulty in buying insurance on property located in blighted or deteriorating urban areas. Basically the plan assures a property owner of physical inspection of property, and a promise to provide fire and allied lines insurance if the property is adequately maintained and if recommended improvements necessary to make the property insurable have been made. Many of these plans have been extended to cover statewide in those states adopting them.

FAMILY AUTOMOBILE POLICY — An automobile policy insuring liability, medical expense, physical damage and uninsured motorists—available only for individually owned private passenger cars and some small trucks. It is somewhat similar to the Combination Automobile Policy, but provides broader coverage.

FARMER'S COMPREHENSIVE PERSONAL LIABILITY INSURANCE — Similar to Comprehensive Personal Liability coverage, but amended to take care of the special accident risks found around the farm. A legal liability or third party policy; i.e., it protects the farmer against bodily injury or property damage claims from others, including, at times, claims from farm employees.

FARMOWNER-RANCHOWNERS POLICY (FO-RO) — A package policy for farming and ranching risks which can be described as a homeowners policy adapted for farm and ranch properties. Basically the policy provides property and liability insurance to which may be added appropriate additional coverages such as animal collision, employers liability, custom farming, etc.

F.A.S. — See FREE ALONG SIDE.

FEDERAL CRIME INSURANCE PROGRAM — Administered by the Federal Insurance Administration to provide limited burglary and robbery coverage for property owners who experience difficulty in buying insurance on property located in blighted or deteriorating urban areas.

FEDERAL INSURANCE ADMINISTRATION — A government office (part of the Department of Housing and Urban Development) handling insurance programs such as the Federal Riot and Civil Commotion Reinsurance Contract (which backs up policies provided by FAIR Plans in force in a number of states), Federal Crime Insurance, and the Federal Flood Insurance Program.

FEDERAL TORT CLAIMS ACT — Historically, the sovereign (government) cannot be sued without its consent. The Federal Tort Claims Act altered this principle and allows persons to sue the United States for personal injury or damage to property under circumstances where the United States, if a private individual, would be liable for such injury or damage.

FELLOW OF THE INSTITUTE OF ACTUARIES (F.I.A.) — A degree or title held by one who has passed examinations and has been admitted to the Institute of Actuaries in England.

FIDELITY BOND — An insurance policy which reimburses an employer for losses resulting from dishonest acts of employees. May be written to cover specific employees or all employees.

FIDUCIARY — A person who occupies a position of trust, especially one who manages the affairs of another. For example, the guardian of a minor is a fiduciary.

FIDUCIARY LIABILITY INSURANCE — Protection for those who administer pension and welfare funds, profit-sharing, and other employee benefit programs against loss for errors and omissions by the administrator. The need for this coverage was created by the Employee Retirement Income Security Act (ERISA) of 1974. Also known as Pension Trust Liability insurance.

FIELD — Territory away from the office.

FIELD REPRESENTATIVE — A company employee whose duties are in the field, generally with the title of special agent or state agent. More commonly known today as a marketing representative or marketing "rep."

FINANCIAL GUARANTY — A guaranty that a sum of money will be paid. A form of bond.

FINANCIAL RESPONSIBILITY CLAUSE — Language in a policy describing coverage required by a FINANCIAL RESPONSIBILITY LAW.

FINANCIAL RESPONSIBILITY LAW — A statute (in force in most states) which requires a motorist to provide evidence of the ability to pay for negligence in causing losses to others from the operation of a motor vehicle. Typically, the evidence furnished is an insurance policy, although most states also permit a bond or cash deposit to be used in lieu of a policy.

FINE ARTS INSURANCE — Coverage on works of arts, usually written by inland marine underwriters on an "all-risks" and a "valued" basis.

FINISHED STOCK — Merchandise of a manufacturer which has been completely processed and is ready for sale.

FIRE — Combustion manifested in light, flame, and heat for useful purposes (FRIENDLY FIRE) or destruction purposes (HOSTILE FIRE). Insurance covers loss from only the latter.

FIRE CLAUSE — A condition in a lease which provides that in case fire should damage the property to some agreed extent, certain agreed modifications in the lease automatically take place.

FIRE DEPARTMENT SERVICE CLAUSE — Sometimes when property is located outside the boundaries of a city or town, the fire department will agree to come to a fire, but a charge is made for it. This clause extends the policy to pay such charges in the event of loss.

FIRE INSURANCE — 1) Covers losses caused by fire, lightning, and removal of insured property from the premises to avoid further loss. All resultant damage such as that done by water and smoke is also covered. Usually supplemented by EXTENDED COVERAGE. 2) A type or line of insurance, as opposed to marine, casualty, or fidelity bonding.

FIRE INSURANCE COMPANY — An insurance company chartered and licensed under the fire insurance provisions of the laws of its home state, as opposed to one under the casualty section. Since the term "fire insurance" has been replaced in many state laws with "property insurance," its legal use is limited, but fire insurance is still applied in a colloquial sense to describe those companies engaged principally in the property insurance business.

50

FIRE MARK — In days gone by (and before public fire departments were created), a small sign or a medallion placed on a building by a fire insurance company which had insured it, to direct its privately contracted fire department to extinguish the blaze. All such departments would respond to a fire alarm, but only the department compensated by the fire mark company would fight the fire. Fire marks are now collectors' items.

FIRE MARSHAL — A public official involved in fire prevention and investigation of fires, particularly where arson is suspected.

FIREPROOF — See FIRE-RESISTIVE.

FIRE-RESISTIVE — The construction of a building with steel and concrete or other noncombustible materials designed to prevent the frequency of fire or to reduce its effect once started. A better term than fireproof, since few materials are incapable of damage or destruction by fire.

FIRE WALL — A wall designed to prevent the spread of a hostile fire. See DIVISION WALL.

FIRST CLASS MAIL INSURANCE — All-risks coverage on bonds, stock certificates and other securities shipped first class mail by banks, trust companies, investment corporations and other firms engaged in security transactions.

FIRST SURPLUS TREATY — As a reinsurance term, first surplus means the amount of liability assumed on a certain risk, which is in addition to the amount which the primary company cares to hold for its net account. A treaty or contract which reinsures this "surplus" on a pro rata basis is called a first surplus treaty. Since there usually is a limit on the amount which may be ceded, there may be second or third surplus treaties to permit the writing of larger direct lines.

FIXED CHARGES — 1) Costs of transacting business, e.g., rents, which are incurred regardless of the amount of business transacted. 2) A term used in business interruption insurance.

FIXTURES — Something attached to real estate which is removable. See FURNITURE AND FIXTURES.

FLAT CANCELLATION — The cancellation of a policy as of the time it attached, with all the premium refunded to the policyholder.

FLAT COMMISSION — A fee for selling and servicing insurance, payable to an agent or broker, which is the same percentage of the premium regardless of the size of the premium. See GRADED COMMISSION.

FLEET — 1) A group of ships or automobiles under common ownership or insured as if they were. 2) A group of companies under common ownership or management.

FLEET POLICY — In automobile insurance, coverage for a number of cars for one owner. In marine insurance, coverage for a number of ships for one owner or manager.

FLOATER — A policy which covers property at many locations, even worldwide and in the course of transit, i.e., the protection "floats around" with the objects insured.

FLOOD — Overflow of water from its natural boundaries. More specifically defined by the National Flood Act of 1968 as "a general and temporary condition of partial or complete inundation of normally dry land areas from (1) the overflow of inland or tidal waters, or (2) the unusual and rapid accumulation or runoff of surface waters from any source."

FLOOD INSURANCE — Coverage against damage done by the rising or overflowing of bodies of water. See NATIONAL FLOOD INSURERS ASSOCIATION.

FLOOR PLAN INSURANCE — Coverage acquired by the financier (finance company or bank) to protect either its interest alone or its joint interest with the merchant, in which a special form is used. Merchants of high valued articles, such as automobiles and expensive household equipment (e.g., refrigerators), often borrow money from finance companies or banks on the collateral of their stock of specifically identified property "on the floor" for sale. See SINGLE INTEREST COVER and CREDIT INSURANCE.

F.O.B. — See FREE ON BOARD.

FOLLOWING THE FORTUNES — A reinsurance principle stipulating that whatever the reinsured may find necessary to do in good faith, in connection with ceded business, is expected to be followed by the reinsurer. Reinsurance is strictly an honorable undertaking, from either side to the other.

FOR ACCOUNT OF WHOM IT MAY CONCERN — A phrase used to protect the interests of others than the "named insureds"—that is, other than the persons actually named in the policy.

FOREIGN COMPANY — In insurance, a company doing business in one state but incorporated in another. A company incorporated in another country is an "alien" company. Some insurance codes, however (Florida, for example), define "foreign company" to include alien companies unless the contrary is stated. Each specific law should be checked for its particular meaning.

FOREIGN CREDIT INSURANCE ASSOCIATION (FCIA) — A group of insurance companies cooperating with the Export-Import Bank of Washington (Eximbank) to provide foreign credit insurance for American exporters and thus assist United States business to become more competitive in foreign trade. Coverage provides for credit and political risks. Headquarters, New York.

FORGERY — False or fraudulent making or altering of a written instrument. Also, the illegal signing of another's name to a document such as a check.

FORM — A document providing the specifics of the insurance issued, either separate unto itself or attached to other descriptive language.

FORTUITOUS CAUSE — An accidental and unexpected cause of loss. A happening by chance.

FOUNDATION EXCLUSION CLAUSE — A clause in a fire policy which states that it does not insure foundations and hence their value may not be used to determine the proper amount of insurance under a coinsurance clause.

FOUNDATION WALL — A masonry wall below the surface which supports a building.

FOUNDERING — Sinking below the surface of water.

FRAME BUILDING — A type of construction in which the outer walls are made of lumber. See BRICK BUILDING and BRICK VENEER.

FRANCHISE CLAUSE — A provision in marine policies that no loss shall be paid by the insurer unless the damage exceeds an agreed amount called the "franchise," but that if the damage equals or exceeds the franchise, the company pays the entire amount. See DEDUCTIBLE.

FRANCHISE INSURANCE — A form of mass merchandising of insurance where policies are sold to members of some common group or association individually on the basis of individual rates, but with some discount based on expense savings. Franchise insurance should be contrasted with group or true group, where premiums are determined for the group on the basis of its own expenses and losses and where all or most of the group are insured.

FRATERNAL INSURANCE — A form of cooperative life or disability insurance sold by certain fraternal organizations (usually as legal reserve insurers) to their members.

FRAUD — Dishonesty.

FREE ALONG SIDE (F.A.S.) — A marine insurance term indicating that, when goods are shipped F.A.S., the shipper agrees to assume all costs and liabilities for loss until the goods are safely on the pier or dock alongside the vessel.

FREE OF CAPTURE AND SEIZURE (FC&S) — A clause which exempts the marine insurance company from paying losses caused by capture or seizure by enemies of a country.

FREE OF PARTICULAR AVERAGE (FPA) — A clause which exempts the company insuring cargo from partial losses, usually limited to apply only if the amount be less than an agreed sum, or if some other described condition exists.

FREE ON BOARD (F.O.B.) — When goods are shipped F.O.B., the shipper is responsible only until the goods have been placed on board the vessel, freight car, truck, or other means of transport. After that the risk belongs to the consignee.

FREE TRADE ZONE — A special section of the New York State Insurance Law that exempts from rate regulation certain risks which develop property-liability policy premiums in excess of $100,000 annually as well as certain other classes of unusual or exotic risks.

FRIENDLY FIRE — A visible flame or glow started voluntarily, under control, and in its intended place. See HOSTILE FIRE.

FRONTING — An arrangement whereby one insurer issues a policy on a risk for and at the request of one or more other insurers with the intent of passing the entire risk by way of reinsurance to the other insurer(s). Such an arrangement may be illegal if the purpose is to frustrate regulatory requirements.

FULL INTEREST ADMITTED (F.I.A.) — An agreement in a policy of marine insurance that the named insured's ownership or right to collect the proceeds of the insurance is agreed to at the inception of risk without further proof of an insurable interest at time of loss.

FULL REPORTING CLAUSE — A clause in many reporting policies that provides for a penalty in the event of loss if the insured has reported less value than required by the policy. Formerly called HONESTY CLAUSE.

FUR FLOATER — An inland marine policy insuring furs and garments containing fur on a scheduled-item basis against all risks, wherever the furs may be.

FURNACE EXPLOSION — A bursting in the fire box of a furnace or boiler, as distinguished from one in the water bearing part. Usually, boiler explosion policies cover the latter, while extended coverage endorsements issued by fire insurance companies cover the former.

FURNITURE AND FIXTURES — In insurance language, usually the contents of a building, excepting merchandise for sale or in the course of manufacture (stock) and excepting machinery. Fixtures are the pieces "fixed," that is, attached to the building.

FURRIERS CUSTOMERS INSURANCE — An inland marine form of insurance in which the customer of a furrier who stores fur garments is insured under a policy arranged by the furrier.

G

GAAP (GENERALLY ACCEPTED ACCOUNTING PRINCIPLES) — A method of reporting the financial results of an insurer more in accordance with the going-concern basis used by other businesses. GAAP assigns income and disbursements to their proper period, as distinguished from the more conservative requirements of statutory accounting affecting insurers. See STATUTORY ACCOUNTING PRINCIPLES.

GAMBLING — Creating risk by agreeing with another to win or lose something on the outcome of a certain event. Insurance is the opposite of gambling: gambling creates risk, while insurance shifts risk already in existence from one party to another.

GAP COVERAGE — An amount of insurance purchased to satisfy the requirement of an excess carrier with respect to underlying insurance. For example, if an excess insurer requires the insured to carry $500,000 of underlying coverage but the primary insurer will write only $300,000, $200,000 is purchased to fill the "gap."

GARAGE POLICY — Protects garage or service station operators for claims alleging bodily injury or property damage caused by the operator's negligence in business operations and the use of automobiles.

GARMENT CONTRACTORS FLOATER — An inland marine form of policy which insures the goods of the manufacturer against physical loss or damage while in transit and during processing or finishing on the premises of other parties serving as contractors or processors.

GARNISHMENT — A court order to a person holding property or money of another not to give it to the owner or anyone else because suit has been filed or other legal steps taken to provide for other courses of action. Money due under insurance policies is sometimes subject to such procedure because of obligations of one to whom the loss would be paid.

GENERAL ADJUSTMENT BUREAU, INC. — A national firm providing extensive loss settling, appraisal, and other services for insurance companies and firms practicing risk retention. Headquarters, New York.

GENERAL AGENT — 1) An independent agent who represents one or more insurers with the authority to appoint sub-agents who report their business through the general agent, who receives an overriding commission for services provided. In some territories a general agent also sells insurance, functioning in others solely as a manager. 2) A title used by some insurers for those of its agents receiving a higher commission rate than its other agents (because of a higher volume of business placed with the insurer); such a general agent normally has no additional authority or responsibility, and the title is used to designate the higher commission rate.

GENERAL AVERAGE — In ocean marine insurance, a loss which is common to all interests (i.e., the hull owners, the cargo owners, and the receivers of the freight and charges, etc.) which may arise due to a peril to the entire venture, which requires a sacrifice or expenditure for the benefit of all. An example is the stranding of the vessel wherein the vessel must engage a tug to remove her from the strand. Without the tug's assistance, all would be lost. The expenses incurred are shared pro rata based on the value of each interest, whether insured or not. See PARTICULAR AVERAGE.

GENERAL COVER — A policy covering property at several locations, the premium for which is determined by averaging the stated amounts of value, which the policyholder is required to report to the company at stated intervals.

GLASS INSURANCE — Coverage against the breakage of glass.

GOOD STUDENT DISCOUNT — A reduced automobile insurance premium is sometimes granted students with high scholastic achievement, because some studies have indicated a relationship between good grades and safe driving.

GOVERNING CLASSIFICATION — In determining rates for compensation insurance, the principal occupation of the insured.

GRACE PERIOD — An amount of time (usually one month) after the life insurance policy's premium due date, during which the policy continues in effect when the premium due is not paid. Many policies which have cash values also provide an automatic premium loan provision, in which part of the cash value is used as a loan to pay the premium due, thereby keeping the policy in force for a longer period. Most state laws require a grace period in life insurance policies.

GRADED COMMISSION — Compensation for selling and servicing insurance, payable to an agent or broker, the percentage of which is dependent on the size of the premium. The higher the premium, the lower the commission percentage. The opposite of FLAT COMMISSION in which the same rate of commission applies for any size of premium.

GRADING OF CITIES AND TOWNS — A 10 category ranking or schedule of public fire protection of cities and towns established in 1916. The grading is currently maintained by the Insurance Services Office for use in making fire insurance rates and to encourage local governments to maintain better fire fighting equipment and personnel. A city or town is ranked in one of the categories by receiving deficiency points for failing to meet established standards under each of these major headings: water supply, fire department, fire service communications, fire safety control, climate, and divergence between fire department and water supply. Town Class 1 is the best class (a city or town having fewer than 501 points), and Town Class 10 is the worst (more than 4500 points).

GROSS EARNINGS FORM — A form of time element business interruption insurance in which the premium consideration is based upon the policyholder's sales less cost of merchandise. This has become a popular form of TIME ELEMENT INSURANCE, particularly for small merchants. See BUSINESS INTERRUPTION INSURANCE.

GROSS LINE — The amount of insurance the company has on a risk, including the amount it may have reinsured. Net line plus reinsurance equals gross line.

GROSS NET PREMIUMS — In company language, gross written premiums less return premiums but not less reinsurance.

GROSS PREMIUM — In company language, the written premium before deducting any premium paid for reinsurance and in some cases before paying any return premium.

GROUP INSURANCE — 1) Insuring a number of persons under a single master contract. The persons have a common sponsor, such as an employer, a union, or an association. 2) "True" group insurance precludes individual underwriting by the insurer, requires the employer to insure all employees if the employer pays any portion of the premium, and allows employees the option of participating in any coverage for which the employees must pay.

GROUP MERCHANDISING — A term often used in a misleading sense to cover all forms of MASS MERCHANDISING. More accurately used to cover the sale of insurance to the members of a particular group or association under a single group contract, where premiums for the participants are determined for the group on the basis of its own expenses and losses and where all or most of the group are insured. See MASS MERCHANDISING and FRANCHISE INSURANCE.

GUARANTY FUND — An amount of money assessed certain insurers in a given state to reimburse policyholders and claimants of an insolvent insurer in that state. The fund may be created before an insolvency occurs (pre-assessment, as in New York) or afterward (post-assessment), and virtually all states now have such protection. See NATIONAL COMMITTEE ON INSURANCE GUARANTY FUNDS.

GUEST STATUTES — In some states, legislation requiring that a guest passenger must prove something higher than ordinary negligence in order to recover from the host driver. Apart from such laws, the guest passenger would have the same rights as any other member of the public and only be required to prove ordinary negligence.

GUIDING PRINCIPLES — Rules agreed on by most insurers for apportioning loss payments among two or more policies covering a given loss.

H

HAIL INSURANCE — See CROP-HAIL INSURANCE.

HANGARKEEPERS LEGAL LIABILITY INSURANCE — Protection for the aircraft hangarkeeper for losses caused by negligence in storing aircraft as a bailee.

HARDWARE — The mechanical electronic and electrical devices comprising a computer. See SOFTWARE.

HARTER ACT — A law, passed by Congress in 1893, which provides that a vessel owner is not responsible for loss or damage caused by faults or errors in navigation, provided the shipowner has taken proper care to see that the ship is in all respects seaworthy and properly manned and equipped.

HAZARD — A condition which may lead to a PERIL, thus creating a loss (e.g., oily rags leading to a fire). See MORAL HAZARD, MORALE HAZARD, PHYSICAL HAZARD.

HEAD OFFICE — See HOME OFFICE.

HEALTH INSURANCE — A broad term describing protection from loss due to illness or injury, resulting in loss of life, loss of earnings, or expenses incurred. Within the broad area of health insurance, there are several major coverages which focus on more specific needs. See, for example, ACCIDENT INSURANCE, DISABILITY INCOME INSURANCE, HOSPITALIZATION INSURANCE, and SICKNESS INSURANCE, among others.

HEALTH MAINTENANCE ORGANIZATION (HMO) — An entity with four essential characteristics: 1) an organized system for providing health care in a geographic area, delivering 2) an agreed upon set of basic and supplemental health maintenance and treatment services to 3) a voluntarily enrolled group of persons 4) for which services the HMO is reimbursed through a predetermined and periodic prepayment made by or on behalf of each person or family unit enrolled in the HMO, without regard to the amounts of actual services provided.

HELD IN TRUST — A clause in property insurance extending the policy to cover property of others held by the insured as a bailee. Such coverage is always qualified by the requirement that the bailee is legally responsible for such property.

HMO — See HEALTH MAINTENANCE ORGANIZATION.

HOLD HARMLESS AGREEMENT — A contractual arrangement in which one party agrees to assume certain liability which otherwise would be borne by the other party. For example, an insurer may wish to pay a loss when it is uncertain whether it may be called upon a second time to some other party. The payee may be asked to execute an agreement whereby the company will be reimbursed or held harmless by the payee if such request should happen. Another example, the principal in a large construction project will frequently demand hold harmless agreements from all subcontractors in respect to claims made against the principal arising out of the subcontractors' negligence. The principal often stipulates the purchase of a liability policy by the subcontractor to support the hold harmless agreement.

HOLD-UP — See ROBBERY.

HOLE-IN-ONE INSURANCE — Coverage which assumes the lucky golfer's traditional responsibilities for buying a round of drinks for everyone in the club.

HOME OFFICE — 1) The principal place of business of a company: the head office or the chief office. 2) The term may be modified to include regional offices in some jurisdictions (Florida) for tax purposes, with a company's principal place of business referred to as its "head" office.

HOMEOWNERS POLICY — A "package" policy for dwelling and contents risks combining fire and allied line coverage with comprehensive personal liability and theft insurance for homeowners and tenants. This policy carries an "indivisible" premium in that the premium is not separately stated or broken down for the various hazards insured against. There are different Homeowners forms, varying in extent of coverage and cost from the "basic" policy (Form No. 1) to the "comprehensive" coverage (Form No. 8).

HONESTY CLAUSE — A former name for the FULL REPORTING CLAUSE in reporting forms of fire policies.

HONORABLE UNDERTAKING — A clause used in some reinsurance treaties, the purpose of which is that the agreement not be defeated by a strict or narrow interpretation of the language in the treaty.

HOSPICE — A program which provides palliative and supportive care for terminally ill patients and their families; either directly or on a consulting basis with the patient's physician or another community agency, such as a visiting nurse association. The entire family is considered the unit of care, and care extends through the mourning process.

HOSPITAL EXPENSE INSURANCE — See HOSPITALIZATION INSURANCE.

HOSPITAL PROFESSIONAL LIABILITY INSURANCE — Protects a hospital against claims for injury resulting from malpractice, professional errors or a mistake of the hospital staff.

HOSPITALIZATION INSURANCE — Reimbursement for certain expenses incurred while being hospitalized due to injury or illness.

HOST LIQUOR LIABILITY INSURANCE — See DRAM LIABILITY INSURANCE.

HOSTILE FIRE — A fire occuring where it is not supposed to be, as distinguished from a FRIENDLY FIRE which occurs in its proper place, such as in a stove or a fireplace. Fire insurance policies do not insure losses caused by friendly fires.

HOUSEHOLD GOODS — The normal contents of a dwelling, such as furniture, clothing, etc.

HOUSEKEEPING — The care and management of property and the provision of equipment and services (as for a home or industrial organization).

HULL — The ship itself as distinguished from its cargo.

HULL SYNDICATE — A group of ocean marine underwriters who insure certain ships or who perform certain functions in the insurance of ships on a joint or cooperative basis to spread the risk automatically and to save expense.

HURRICANE — A violent cyclonic windstorm covering a large area. It usually originates at sea, with winds circulating at tremendous velocity around a "center," which in itself moves fairly slowly. It differs from a tornado, which may be more violent, in that the area of involvement is always extremely large. A typhoon is the Pacific and Indian Ocean version of a hurricane. See TYPHOON.

I

I.C.C. ENDORSEMENT — See INTERSTATE COMMERCE ENDORSEMENT TO MOTOR TRUCK CARGO POLICIES.

IMPAIRED CAPITAL — The capital of an insurance company is said to be impaired if its liabilities, subtracted from its assets, leave less than the stated amount of capital. Most states have statutes outlining procedures to be taken by the insurance superintendent or commissioner in the event of such impairment. The word "impaired," standing alone, has specific statutory meaning in state laws, which may vary from state to state. Relevant state laws should be checked for meaning and effect.

IMPLIED WARRANTY — An indirect expression or inference, not in writing, by the policyholder that certain conditions exist or will be met (e.g., that a building is not on fire when insured, or that a vessel is seaworthy).

IMPROVEMENTS AND BETTERMENTS — Additions made to real estate enhancing its value and amounting to more than mere repairs or replacement of waste. When made by a tenant, such additions are normally included in the tenant's own property insurance.

IN FORCE PREMIUMS — The original premiums paid on all policies not yet expired, as distinguished from UNEARNED PREMIUMS.

IN KIND — Replacement of damaged, destroyed, or lost property with other property instead of cash.

INCENDIARY — 1) The person who deliberately sets fire to a property. 2) A destructive fire intentionally set.

INCHMAREE — A clause used in ocean marine policies to identify additional named perils beyond the basic marine perils. In the more recent hull insurance policies, the clause is now identified as the "additional perils" clause. The original clause was identified by reason of a lawsuit brought in 1887 by the owners of a ship named "Inchmaree" which resulted in the adoption of the clause by marine underwriters.

INCREASE IN HAZARD — The standard fire insurance policy is suspended from liability while the hazard in a risk has been increased beyond what was contemplated at the time the policy was written. For example, if a dwelling house, insured as such, should be occupied for manufacturing purposes without getting consent from the insurer for such increase in hazard, the company would not have to pay a loss as long as the manufacturing condition existed.

INCURRED EXPENSE — A cost of administering insurance which has happened, whether or not paid.

INCURRED BUT NOT REPORTED (IBNR) — The liability for future payments on losses which have already occurred but have not yet been reported to the insurer. This definition may be extended to include expected future development on claims already reported.

INCURRED LOSSES — 1) Events which have happened and which will cause claims to be made to insurers. 2) The total amount shown in an insurer's operating statement as its obligations for policy claims, whether or not paid, during a given period (usually one year). The composition of incurred losses in such a total is derived by this formula: losses paid during the year, plus loss reserves existing at the end of the year, minus loss reserves existing at the beginning of the year.

INDEMNIFY — To pay for loss suffered.

INDEMNITOR — In surety bonds, a person or company entering into a written agreement with a surety to hold that surety harmless from any loss or expense it may incur on a bond issued on behalf of another.

INDEMNITY COMPANY — Usually a company which confines its writings to the classes defined as "casualty," as opposed to fire or marine. The term is becoming meaningless in these days, when fire companies are writing casualty lines and indemnity or casualty companies are writing fire lines.

INDEPENDENT ADJUSTER — One who adjusts losses on behalf of companies but is not employed by any one. Paid by fee for each loss adjusted, as distinguished from a "staff" adjuster who is paid a salary by one company for work performed. Not to be confused with PUBLIC ADJUSTER, who represents the policyholder instead of the company.

INDEPENDENT AGENT — A property-liability insurance producer who sells insurance as an independent contractor while representing one or more insurers of that agent's choosing on a commission basis, owning the expiration records of customers served. The independent status is further illustrated by the selling functions performed, which are not directed by the insurer, as would be the case if the agent were an employee. Those functions include contacting prospective insureds, effecting insurance, issuing policies, collecting premiums (in many or most cases), settling some losses of small amounts, and generally representing the insurers in the agent's community as a part of the AMERICAN AGENCY SYSTEM. By contrast, the direct writing insurer directs the selling functions of its agents, known as exclusive agents, and owns the expiration records. See AMERICAN AGENCY SYSTEM, DIRECT WRITER, and EXCLUSIVE AGENT.

INDEPENDENT INSURANCE AGENTS OF AMERICA (IIAA) — Formerly the National Association of Insurance Agents, a large trade association whose purpose is to protect the business interests of its members, who are also members of state associations.

INDIRECT DAMAGE — Loss resulting from, or as a consequence of, an insured direct loss. Examples: loss of business income to a firm from direct damage to the firm's premises; loss of business income to a supplier of a firm whose premises are destroyed; loss of income to a family from death of the family's breadwinner.

INDIVIDUAL RISK PREMIUM MODIFICATION RATING PLAN — A program whereby equitable rates or premiums can be developed for large premium package risks by taking into consideration factors likely to affect future losses and expenses. Expense modification is based on the fact that handling costs for large risks may vary from the average. Risk modification recognizes special characteristics, other than those considered in the determination of the basic rate, which would improve the risk. This flexible rating approach, in effect for casualty insurance for many years, was extended to the remaining property and liability lines in 1966.

INDUSTRIAL INSURANCE — Insurance (usually life insurance) written in small amounts, the premium for which is payable in frequent installments (usually weekly or monthly) and collected by an agent known as a DEBIT AGENT. The payment frequency and collection facilities were designed to accommodate workers at industrial factories, decades ago, who were paid weekly.

INDUSTRIAL PROPERTY FORM — A package coverage designated for manufacturers and processors, insuring against loss or damage to building and personal property at two or more stated locations by specified perils such as fire, windstorm, explosion, burglary or robbery, etc. May be extended by endorsement to convert to "all risks" basis, including transit risks. Not available to certain manufacturing and processing risks for which special policies have been designed. A form somewhat similar to the MANU-FACTURERS OUTPUT POLICY.

INDUSTRIAL RISK INSURERS — A consortium of major stock property and casualty insurers formed to write large, highly protected risks and to provide fire laboratory facilities and engineering services. The organization was formed in 1975 by the merger of the Factory Insurance Association and the Oil Insurance Association.

INFLATION GUARD ENDORSEMENT — Language which may be added to a Homeowners Policy for an additional premium to extend the coverage by increasing the limits of liability quarterly (by 1%, 1¼%, or some fixed amount) to offset inflation.

INHERENT EXPLOSION — Explosion caused by the normal processes of a risk (as opposed to one caused by external causes), e.g., a dust explosion in a grain elevator.

INHERENT VICE — The characteristics of any physical property which are expected to cause deterioration or damage to that property without outside help, e.g., milk sours eventually, and wooden houses depreciate over time. Excluded by most insurance policies.

INITIAL PREMIUM — A tentative charge made at the start of certain policies which is subsequently adjusted, at expiration or after certain information has been developed. Also known as DEPOSIT PREMIUM.

INJURY — An act which damages or destroys a person or property.

INLAND MARINE — 1) The insurance of property (generally on an all-risk basis) which is in the course of transportation or is of such a nature that it may easily be transported. Also includes some risks at fixed locations considered "instruments of transportation or communication"; such as bridges, tunnels, neon signs, street clocks, etc., which were accepted as inland marine by custom. 2) Originally meant the insurance of goods in transit "inland," instead of at sea, by underwriters who specialized in ocean marine insurance.

INNKEEPERS LEGAL LIABILITY — Hotel and motel operators are legally liable for the safekeeping of guests' property. Extent of this liability is established by various state laws. Innkeepers legal liability policy insures against this liability imposed by law, usually with a limit of $1,000 for any one guest, and with an appropriate aggregate limit.

INNOCENT CAPACITY — The amount of insurance offered the public by inexperienced insurers or reinsurers.

INSOLVENCY CLAUSE — Required by law to be included in reinsurance contracts, this clause holds the reinsurer liable for payments under a treaty, even though the reinsured company in that treaty has become insolvent.

INSOLVENCY FUND — See GUARANTY FUND.

INSPECTION — A visual or physical examination of a property to determine whether it is an acceptable risk for insurance. See CREDIT REPORT.

INSPECTION BUREAU — 1) In some states, a rating bureau. 2) An organization which inspects risks and makes surveys for the use of companies in their underwriting.

INSPECTION SLIP — The report of an inspector on the characteristics of the insured property.

INSPECTOR — One who looks at risks and reports on their acceptability for cover. In marine insurance, an inspector is a "surveyor."

INSTALLATION RISK INSURANCE — Protection for the installer of equipment against loss by specified perils to property in the course of installation.

INSTALLMENT PREMIUM — The payment of certain premiums may be made by the policyholder in installments.

INSTALLMENT SALES FLOATER — Protects the seller of property in possession of the purchaser (for which payments by the purchaser have not been completed) against loss caused by insured perils to the seller's remaining financial interest. Also known as CONDITIONAL SALES FLOATER.

INSTITUTIONAL POLICY — A package policy forming a part of the Special Multi-Peril Policy program applicable to institutional buildings (e.g., buildings occupied by educational, religious, sanatory, charitable, governmental or nonprofit organizations). Basically the policy covers fire and allied lines, and liability and can be extended for most additional required coverages such as boiler and machinery, burglary and robbery, fidelity, business interruption, etc.

INSURABLE INTEREST — A potential for financial loss from a certain event which a person must have before acquiring insurance against that event. The event may be illustrated by the following, among others: the destruction of property owned (In-Force insurance), the incurring of legal liability for negligence in causing loss to others (in liability insurance), the compliance with law (in workers compensation insurance), the loss or impairment of human life value (in life insurance, disability insurance, annuities), or expenses fortuitously incurred (in hospitalization insurance). In life insurance, the applicant of the policy must suffer a financial loss, or the loss of love and affection, by the death of the insured.

INSURABLE RISK — Any subject matter eligible for insurance. While the law does not specify minimum criteria (except occasionally by regulation that the size of any risk insured and the amount of premium writings by an insurer be related to its financial strength), and textbook writers disagree on essential criteria, the following are probably desirable: 1) enough relatively similar exposure units should be insured to permit the operation of the Law of Large Numbers (unless reinsurance is used by the insurer); 2) losses insured should be measurable and accidental to the insured (to prevent intentional losses); and 3) risks taken should not threaten the insurer with a catastrophe (unless reinsurance is used) because of their centralized location or other condition.

INSURANCE — The transfer of risk (chance of loss) from one party (the insured) to another party (the insurer), in which the insurer promises (usually specified in a written contract) to pay the insured (or others on the insured's behalf) an amount of money (or services, or both) for economic losses sustained from an unexpected (accidental) event, during a period of time for which the insured makes a premium payment to the insurer.

INSURANCE ACCOUNTING AND STATISTICAL ASSOCIATION (IASA) — An international organization to promote the study, research and development of modern theory, practice and procedure as applied to insurance accounting and statistics. Headquarters, Durham, North Carolina.

INSURANCE ADVERTISING CONFERENCE (IAC) — A trade association of those in charge of insurance company advertising.

INSURANCE AGENTS AND BROKERS ERRORS AND OMISSIONS INSURANCE — Protects an agent or broker against claims for negligent acts, errors or omissions in the conduct of business.

66

INSURANCE COMMISSIONER — A state official charged with enforcing the state's laws governing insurance, in some states appointed by the governor but elected in 11 others. Also referred to in some states as superintendent of insurance or director of insurance.

INSURANCE COMPANY — An organization chartered by state law to operate as an insurer in certain of the principal types of insurance, viz., life, fire, marine, casualty and surety. Reciprocals and Lloyds syndicates permitted under many state laws are not companies, nor are they corporations.

INSURANCE COMPANY EDUCATION DIRECTORS SOCIETY (ICEDS) — An organization of education and training directors from all sections of the insurance industry. The society aims to improve training methods and techniques for both company personnel and agents.

INSURANCE CRIME PREVENTION INSTITUTE (ICPI) — Serves casualty insurers for the investigation of fraudulent insurance claims other than for accident and health or workers compensation, and provides a deterrent to such losses. Headquarters, Westport, Connecticut.

INSURANCE DEPARTMENT — That department of a state government which has charge of enforcing the laws governing insurance. See COMMISSIONER OF INSURANCE.

INSURANCE EXCHANGES — Exchanges established by law in New York, Illinois, and Florida (and considered elsewhere) to provide facilities at a fixed location patterned after Lloyd's of London. Through insurance exchanges, buyers can secure insurance from insurers generally in the form of underwriting syndicates, which are members of the exchange. See NEW YORK INSURANCE EXCHANGE and LLOYD'S OF LONDON.

INSURANCE GUARANTY (INSOLVENCY) ACT — Legislation enacted in many states providing for assessments on insurance companies to reimburse policyholders and claimants of insolvent insurers. See GUARANTY FUND.

INSURANCE HALL OF FAME — An institution at Ohio State University recognizing individuals who have made outstanding contributions to insurance thought and practice anywhere at any time.

INSURANCE INFORMATION INSTITUTE — A public relations organization supported by several hundred property and liability insurance companies, both stock and mutual. Provides extensive literature to high schools throughout the country and the public in furthering its purpose of improving public understanding of property-liability insurance.

INSURANCE INSOLVENCY ACT — See INSURANCE GUARANTY ACT.

INSURANCE INSTITUTE OF AMERICA INC. (IIA) — An educational organization which sets standards and gives examinations for diplomas or fellowships in general insurance, loss adjusting, underwriting, management, and risk management. Headquarters, Malvern, Pa.

INSURANCE INSTITUTE FOR HIGHWAY SAFETY — An independent, nonprofit scientific organization established and supported by the insurance companies. Its research identifies, evaluates and develops ways to reduce human and economic damage resulting from the use of motor vehicles. The Institute also seeks to make the results of their studies known to the widest possible audience, including substantial input to federal policymakers. Headquarters in Washington, D.C.

INSURANCE REGULATORY INFORMATION SYSTEM — See NAIC INSURANCE REGULATORY INFORMATION SYSTEM.

INSURANCE SERVICES OFFICE (ISO) — A voluntary, nonprofit association of property and casualty insurance companies providing a great variety of services on a national basis. Among its operations are rating, statistical, actuarial and policy form services for all classes of property and casualty business. The association also functions, as provided by law, as an insurance rating organization. In addition, where applicable, ISO acts as an advisory organization or as a statistical agent. Established in 1971 by the consolidation of numerous associations and bureaus performing these services for separate classes of business and in various parts of the country. Headquarters, New York.

INSURANCE SOCIETY OF NEW YORK, INC. — A nonprofit organization founded in 1901 for educational purposes. Its earliest contribution was the formation of its insurance library, today the world's largest collection of insurance literature. In 1917 it started insurance instruction, which became in 1947 The School of Insurance, which was converted in 1962 to the fully accredited degree-granting institution, THE COLLEGE OF INSURANCE.

INSURANCE SUPERINTENDENT — See COMMISSIONER OF INSURANCE.

INSURED — The person(s) or party(ies) protected by an insurance policy, synonymous with assured. Some property-liability policies distinguish between the named insured and other insureds. See POLICYHOLDER and NAMED INSURED.

INSURER — The insurance company or other organization (such as a syndicate, pool or association) providing insurance coverage and services. See INSURANCE.

INSURING CLAUSE — That portion of a policy which describes the risk which the insurer has agreed to assume.

INSUROR — A term adopted and used by some agents to enhance their public image as persons who represent insurers in effecting contracts of insurance between insurers and insureds. As such, insuror may be considered a misnomer when confused with insurer, which is recognized in statutory law as the party to an insurance contract which undertakes to indemnify for losses incurred by, or to provide services to, the other party to the insurance contract, the insured. Thus, an insurer is a risk-bearing party in an insurance contract, while an insuror is not. Two state associations of insurance agents use insuror in their title—Tennessee and Colorado.

INTEREST — The subject of insurance, i.e., the property insured or the loss against which the insurance company agrees to indemnify. See INSURABLE INTEREST.

INTEREST POLICY — A policy which insures someone who has an interest in the described property but need not be the holder of full title to it. The New York standard form of fire policy adopted in 1943 is an interest policy, whereas the older forms were not.

INTERIM RATES — Temporary insurance prices, specified by a state insurance department for an insurer which has no legally effective rates otherwise, as a result of the commissioner's disapproval of its rates. The commissioner may require that a specified portion of premiums received during such interim period be placed in escrow until new rates become effective.

INTERINSURANCE EXCHANGE — A group of persons who agree to share each other's losses. An unincorporated mutual. Also known as "reciprocal exchange."

INTERMEDIARY — One who arranges reinsurance between companies. A reinsurance broker.

INTERNATIONAL ASSOCIATION OF HEALTH UNDERWRITERS — A trade association composed of insurance companies writing health insurance. The purpose is to foster proper practice in the marketing of these products and to create good public relations.

INTERSTATE COMMERCE — The Constitution of the United States places the regulation of commerce between the several states (interstate commerce) under the supervision of the Federal Government. Until the decision of the Supreme Court in 1944 in the South-Eastern Underwriters Association Case, insurance had been held not to be commerce and therefore not interstate commerce. That decision changed the whole outlook so that today the business is subject to such regulation as the Congress chooses to exert, "to the extent that the states are not regulating insurance."

INTERSTATE COMMERCE ENDORSEMENT TO MOTOR TRUCK CARGO POLICIES (ICC ENDORSEMENT) — Broadens the policy coverage to conform to ICC requirements with respect to a carrier's liability for customers' goods.

INVENTORY — A list of one's possessions, usually personal possessions as distinguished from "real" possessions. Also the stock in trade of a business.

INVESTMENT INCOME — That part of a company's income that is derived from its assets (stocks, bonds, mortgages, real estate) as opposed to its underwriting (risk-taking) activities.

INVOLUNTARY ASSOCIATIONS — Those industry or industry-related organizations operating under an industry or governmental program to supply insurance needs for what is purported to be an unfilled or residue market.

IRIS — See NAIC INSURANCE REGULATORY INFORMATION SYSTEM.

J

JETTISON — In ocean marine insurance, the voluntary throwing overboard of part of the cargo or gear of the vessel to lighten the load and save the vessel from conditions of stress at sea. Because the jettison was done for the entire venture, the owner of the jettisoned goods is entitled to a general average, i.e., the loss is shared by all interests in the voyage (vessel, freight, and the owners of the cargo not thrown over). See GENERAL AVERAGE and SACRIFICE.

JEWELERS BLOCK INSURANCE — Broad policies insuring jewelers against all loss to their stock in trade. Generally considered to be a type of inland marine insurance.

JEWELRY FLOATER — An inland marine policy insuring jewelry wherever it may be.

JOINT UNDERWRITING ASSOCIATIONS (or PLANS) — See AUTOMOBILE INSURANCE PLANS.

JUMBO LINE — Any larger-than-usual submission to an underwriter.

K

KART OWNERS POLICY — Not for the nonhazardous golf cart, but a special liability coverage for its more dangerous relative often used for racing. Covers bodily injury and property damage legal liability arising from ownership, maintenance or use of the kart, including racing, but only on private property.

KEETON-O'CONNELL PLAN — A "no-fault" plan for compensating automobile accident victims for their loss of wages and medical expenses, etc., without the usual legal proof of negligence. Devised by Professors Robert E. Keeton and Jeffrey O'Connell. See NO-FAULT AUTOMOBILE INSURANCE.

KIDNAP/RANSOM INSURANCE — Originated as a policy for financial institutions, mainly banks, and tailored to meet the standard kidnap procedure: forcing the bank to withdraw the ransom money from their vaults and deliver it to a designated place before release of the banker or family. The recent rash of kidnapping on an international scale involving a variety of corporations has created a heavy demand for a broadened coverage. At this time there is a limited market, a disinclination to write in certain countries, and no standardization in rates. The insurance covers named employees for individual or aggregate amounts, with deductibles requiring the insured to participate in about 10% of any loss. Not an easy class to underwrite. Personal accident coverage for kidnap victims is sometimes available.

L

LANDLORD'S PROTECTIVE LIABILITY — If an owner of a property leases the entire premises to others who assume full control, the chance of being held liable for accidents occurring on the premises is diminished. The owner can insure the liability as "landlord's protective liability," at rates less than for the normal "owners, landlords and tenants" form of policy.

LAPSE — The termination of a policy for nonpayment of premium, used more commonly in life insurance. If the insurance contract becomes void for other reasons, it is also said to have lapsed.

LARCENY — Theft of personal property. Modern criminal laws include obtaining property under false pretenses and embezzlement, which common law did not include in theft.

LARGE RISK — An object of insurance, the loss of which would seriously affect the operating results of the insurer or the local insurance market over a period of years.

LAW OF LARGE NUMBERS — A mathematical concept which postulates that the more times an event is repeated (in insurance, the larger the number of homogeneous exposure units), the more predictable the outcome becomes. In a classic example, the more times one flips a coin, the more likely that the results will be 50% heads, 50% tails.

LAWYERS PROFESSIONAL LIABILITY INSURANCE — Protects an attorney or law firm against claims for negligent acts, errors or omission in the performance of professional legal services.

LAY UP REFUND — In a policy insuring a vessel, the company may agree to refund a certain proportion of the premium in the event that the vessel be laid up, that is, not in use. Also applicable to automobiles.

LAY UP WARRANTY — A provision in a policy insuring a vessel whereby the policyholder agrees that the vessel will not be in use at certain times.

LEASEHOLD INSURANCE — Protection against the lessee's (tenant's) loss of value when a lease is cancelled because a fire or other peril renders the property unusable, the value being the excess of the rental value of the property over the rental payable in the lease. The insurance against the loss of such value is "leasehold" insurance against whatever perils it may be written. More popular with long leases in periods of rising rental values.

LEGAL EXPENSE INSURANCE — Insurance covering legal costs, written generally on a group basis. Includes the indemnification through providing agreed legal services as well as the payment of money to compensate the insured for costs. Also referred to as prepaid legal insurance.

LEGAL LIABILITY — Liability imposed by law, as opposed to liability arising from an agreement or contract.

LIABILITY — 1) An obligation imposed by law or equity. 2) Money owed or expected to be owed. In an insurance company financial statement, the two columns it contains are its "assets" (or the amounts it owns) and the "liabilities" (or the amount it owes or expects to owe). Liabilities generally are defined by state statute or insurance department regulation for use in the Annual Statement of an insurer. The term is also defined by other regulatory officials for special purposes, such as the Securities and Exchange Commission.

LIABILITY INSURANCE — Protection which pays sums that an insured is legally obligated to pay, or that the insurer has agreed to pay, as damages to others as a result of the insured's negligence. May cover bodily injury to another or damage to property of another. See PROPERTY AND CASUALTY INSURANCE.

LIBEL — 1) To publish defamatory statements about another. The general distinction between libel and slander is that the first must be in writing or similar permanent form, while the latter is oral. The distinction at law is not as simple. 2) In maritime law, the word for a legal action directed against a ship.

LIBEL INSURANCE — Insurance against claims arising from purported libel, slander, defamation, etc. Bought principally by those engaged in the publishing or advertising business and radio and television. Now commonly included in the personal injury endorsement of commercial liability policies.

LICENSE — 1) The certificate of authority granted by a state to insurance companies, agents, brokers, and (in some states) loss adjusters as a permit to engage in the insurance business within the state. 2) The fee or tax paid to secure a certificate of authority (e.g., insurance accounting terminology refers to an insurer's "premium taxes, licenses, and fees").

LICENSE AND PERMIT BOND — A surety bond often required by municipalities and other public authorities to indemnify them against loss from breach of any regulation or ordinance under which the license or permit is issued.

LIGHTNING CLAUSE — A clause formerly attached to a fire insurance policy extending the coverage to include damage done by lightning. Since the fire policy now covers lightning damage, the term is of historical interest only.

LIMIT or LIMIT OF LIABILITY — According to the terms of a given policy, the most an insurer will pay for any one loss. See AGGREGATE LIMIT.

LINE — 1) Either the limit of insurance to be written on a class of risk which a company has fixed for itself (line limit), or the actual amount which it has accepted on a single risk or other unit. 2) A class or type of insurance (fire, marine, or casualty, among others), also known as LINE OF BUSINESS. 3) The word "line" in reinsurance usually pertains to surplus reinsurance and means the amount of the reinsured's retention as respects each risk. Thus, reference to a "two-line" reinsurance treaty pertains to a treaty which affords reinsurance for 200% of the reinsured's retention.

73

LINE CARD — 1) When a risk does not appear on the Sanborn map, fire insurance companies are accustomed to list the details of it on a location card to determine if and when the company is offered another line on the same piece of property. 2) In an agent's office, the card on which all the insurance sold to one customer is listed.

LINE GUIDE — A list of the maximum amounts of insurance which a company is prepared to write on various classes of risks: it usually includes a suggested net retention for each class of risk, and is used to instruct an insurer's agents and underwriters. Also known as a Line Sheet.

LINE OF BUSINESS — The general classification of insurance written by insurers, i.e., fire, allied lines, and homeowners, among others.

LINE SHEET — Another name for LINE GUIDE.

LIQUOR LICENSE BOND — Any bond required by federal, state or municipal authorities to comply with regulations for the handling and sale of liquor.

LIQUOR LIABILITY INSURANCE — See DRAM SHOP LIABILITY INSURANCE.

LIVESTOCK INSURANCE — Covering horses and other cattle against injury and death. Much of it is written by specialty companies which write only this one class.

LLOYDS — A group, acting as individuals, to share in making contracts of insurance. See LLOYD'S OF LONDON and AMERICAN LLOYDS.

LLOYD'S BROKER — A broker accredited to deal with Underwriters at Lloyd's, London, the rules of which do not permit the placement of insurance other than through such a broker.

LLOYD'S OF LONDON — A collection of individuals who assume policy obligations as the individual obligations of each. The formal name is Underwriters at Lloyd's, London. Also, Lloyd's of London is a service organization which provides a central marketplace and ancillary services (such as policywriting, accounting, inspections, and adjusting) for its underwriting members and its brokers.

LLOYD'S REGISTER — A catalogue of ships which describes each vessel, its dimensions, age, place of construction, registry, ownership, etc. A necessary tool of the ocean marine underwriters. Similar information published by the American Bureau of Shipping.

LLOYD'S SYNDICATE — A group of underwriters at Lloyd's of London whose business is handled by an underwriter on behalf of all in the group.

LOADING — 1) As an insurance term, an amount added to an insurance "pure risk" rate applicable to a class of risk, either to compensate the insurer for additional hazard present with an individual risk, for the insurer's expenses, or for both. 2) In marine language, the process of placing merchandise or cargo on board a ship or vehicle.

LOCAL AGENT — The person in direct contact with the public as a licensed representative of an insurer for selling insurance. A local agent is to be distinguished from "state" agent or "special" agent.

LOCAL BOARD — A trade association of local agents banded together to discuss their business, exchange ideas, and promote good practices.

LONG TAIL — A colloquialism referring to the lengthy period of time between the occurrence of an event giving rise to a third-party claim and the claim itself. While this lengthy period is common to all kinds of third-party claims, as opposed to direct damage claims, it is most pronounced in professional liability insurance written on an "occurrence" basis, as opposed to a "claims-made" basis. See CLAIMS-MADE.

LOSS — 1) The amount the insurer is required to pay because of a happening against which it has insured. 2) A happening that causes the company to pay (e.g., any reduction in quantity, quality, or value of insured property resulting from an insured peril). 3) The over-all financial result of some operation, as opposed to "profit." 4) The amount suffered by a person or property, with or without insurance.

LOSS CONSTANT — Used mainly in workers compensation insurance, a flat charge added to the premium of small risks to offset the higher loss ratios produced by such risks. Also used in some states in fire insurance premiums for low valued dwelling risks to offset the higher loss ratios they produce.

LOSS DEPARTMENT — The personnel of a company dealing with claims or losses. In casualty operations the department is referred to as the claim department. See CLAIM DEPARTMENT.

LOSS EXECUTIVES ASSOCIATION — A group of loss department executives of stock insurance companies formed to discuss loss and adjustment problems.

LOSS EXPOSURE — Loss potential. See EXPOSURE.

LOSS OF USE INSURANCE — Insurance which compensates the policyholder for inability to use property destroyed or damaged by an insured peril. For example, if a car is stolen, loss of use insurance will pay or contribute to the cost of hiring a substitute car.

LOSS PAYABLE CLAUSE — A condition in a policy whereby the company may be directed by the policyholder to pay any loss due the policyholder to some other party designated in the policy. Usually the payment is made by check or draft payable to both the insured and the designated payee.

LOSS POCKET — A folder in which are placed all the documents pertaining to a certain loss.

LOSS PREVENTION — Inspection and engineering work on insured risks to help remove potential causes of loss. Loss prevention work applies to both property and casualty insurance and is sometimes called "safety engineering." Also known as ACCIDENT PREVENTION.

LOSS RATIO — Losses incurred expressed as a percentage of premiums (most commonly earned premiums, although written premiums are sometimes used).

LOSS REPORT — A written statement made by an agent, an insured, a claimant, or a beneficiary containing details of the claim being made under an insurance policy.

LOSS RESERVE — An estimate of the amount an insurer expects to pay for reported and estimated claims. May include amounts for loss adjustment expenses. See INCURRED BUT NOT REPORTED and INCURRED LOSSES.

LOSSES INCURRED — See INCURRED LOSSES.

LOSSES OUTSTANDING — Losses which have been incurred but not yet paid.

LOSSES PAID — The sum of losses for which money has been disbursed as opposed to losses incurred, which includes losses outstanding but still unpaid.

LOST OR NOT LOST — A clause used in ocean marine insurance that provides the insurer will pay even if the loss insured against has occurred prior to the effecting of the insurance. The company would, of course, not be liable if the policyholder knew that the loss had occurred when ordering the insurance. A ship could easily be lost or damaged and the owner not know it until later, during which time the owner might want to insure it, which is possible with this clause.

LOST POLICY RELEASE — An agreement signed by the policyholder relieving the insurer from liability under an insurance contract which has been lost, misplaced, or is otherwise unavailable.

M

MACHINERY BREAKDOWN INSURANCE — See BOILER AND MACHINERY INSURANCE.

MAIL-ORDER INSURANCE — Purchasing insurance in response to solicitation by mail from insurers, a practice used by some insurers in marketing life, health, and automobile insurance.

MAJOR MEDICAL INSURANCE — A policy designed to reimburse the insured for excess medical expenses in and out of the hospital. The policy usually includes a deductible, a co-insurance clause, and an aggregate limit.

MALPRACTICE — Improper actions or failure to exercise proper skill by a professional or others involved with the care of the human body; such as a physician, dentist, blood bank, etc. Malpractice insurance is a form of liability coverage against such mistakes. See ERRORS AND OMISSIONS INSURANCE.

MANUAL — A book or series of books (as many as 20 for commercial lines) which contain rules and other information necessary for local offices of insurers, agents, and brokers to write and service policies of insurance: underwriting rules, rates, tables for return premiums, deductibles, relativity tables, minimum premiums, etc.

MANUAL RATE — A charge for a unit of insurance set forth in a manual of instructions.

MANUFACTURERS AND CONTRACTORS LIABILITY INSURANCE (M&C) — Insurance of liability arising from business operations, including ownership and maintenance of premises. Applicable mainly to persons or corporations engaged in manufacturing, construction and installation work. Policies always exclude automobile liability.

MANUFACTURERS OUTPUT POLICY — "All-risk" property coverage for personal property of industrial firms away from the insured's own manufacturing premises.

MAP — See SANBORN MAP.

MAP CLERK — One who records the company's property lines on the Sanborn Map or other records of the company's liability. In the past, being a map clerk was the first step to becoming a fire underwriter, but now the daily practice of mapping fire insurance liability has almost ceased.

MARINE DEFINITION — See NATIONWIDE MARINE DEFINITION.

MARINE INSURANCE — One of major divisions of insurance (life, health, property, marine, casualty, surety), primarily written for property in transit. If by sea, "ocean" marine (or "wet" marine); otherwise, "inland" marine.

MARINE PERILS — The perils which are insured against in a policy of ocean marine insurance. The wording of the marine policy is the result of several hundred years of careful study, judicial interpretation, and precedent, and thus such perils have attained an exact and definite meaning in marine insurance.

MARINE SYNDICATES — Groups of insurance underwriters which act through a manager to insure certain ocean marine classes of business, See SYNDICATE.

MARINE LAW — See ADMIRALTY COURTS.

MARGIN ACCOUNT INSURANCE — A form of credit life coverage, usually written on a group basis, to protect both stock broker and stock purchaser against loss from the death of the purchaser while monies are owed for stock acquired on margin (or with partial payment).

MARKET VALUE CLAUSE — A clause in which the insurer agrees that the amount it will pay in the event of loss shall be the value of the destroyed merchandise "on the market," i.e., the amount which could have been realized by selling the merchandise. Obviously this includes the seller's profit, therefore the clause is used with caution to avoid the creation of a moral hazard.

MARKETING REPRESENTATIVE — See FIELD REPRESENTATIVE.

MASS MARKETING — See MASS MERCHANDISING.

MASS MERCHANDISING — A marketing plan or technique whereby a group of persons insure with one company, usually at lower than standard premiums because of expense economy to the insurer. Premiums are usually collected and remitted to the insurer by a controlling body, such as an employer, a labor union, or a trade association.

MASTER — The commander of a commercial vessel. Popularly, the "captain," but the term in admiralty law and marine insurance is "master."

MASTER POLICY — An insurance policy, used in group insurance, that covers a group of persons to whom certificates of insurance are issued as their evidence of individual coverage under the policy. The two parties to the master policy are the sponsor of the group and the insurer.

MATERIAL FACT — Information having objective reality which influences an insurer in granting or not granting insurance coverage.

MAXIMUM FORESEEABLE LOSS (MFL) — The anticipated maximum property fire loss that could result, given unusual or the worst circumstances with respect to the non-functioning of protective features (e.g., firewalls, sprinklers, and a responsive fire department, among others), as opposed to PROBABLE MAXIMUM LOSS (PML), which is a similar valuation but is made under the assumption that such protective features function normally.

MAXIMUM POSSIBLE LOSS (MPL) — The largest percentage of the insured property which could possibly be destroyed by the insured perils. Normally this amount would be all the property within the four walls of a structure plus loss to adjacent property due to its proximity. An MPL estimate is invariably the ultimate in pessimism, but it is a most important concept in underwriting large risks in order to compute rates and to understand the need for capacity, as well as to appreciate all exposures. Two other expressions used from time to time, AMOUNT SUBJECT and MAXIMUM FORESEE-ABLE LOSS (MFP), have substantially the same meaning as MPL.

McCARRAN-FERGUSON ACT — Enacted on March 9, 1945, a law by which Congress granted authority to the states to continue to tax and regulate the business of insurance (after the insurance business in 1944 had been held by the Supreme Court in a landmark case to be commerce, and therefore subject to federal regulation whenever subject to interstate regulation). See SOUTHEASTERN UNDER-WRITERS ASSOCIATION. The Act provided further that the antitrust laws should not apply to the extent the business of insurance is regulated by the states, except for coercion, intimidation, and boycott. Also known as Public Law 15 (79th Congress, 1945. Mc-Carran-Ferguson Regulation Act: 15 U.S.C. 1011-15).

MECHANICS PERMIT — A clause in a policy granting permission to employ workers, i.e., mechanics, in and around the risk, since their work may increase the exposure. Permission is usually automatically included for such repairs and alterations which are necessary for the maintenance of the premises.

MEDICAL MALPRACTICE — See MALPRACTICE.

MEDICAID — Federal government assistance to states providing medical care for the needy, created by the 1965 amendments to the Social Security Act.

MEDICAL EXPENSE INSURANCE — Insurance providing for payment of medical, surgical, and hospital expenses.

MEDICAL PAYMENTS INSURANCE — Protection to pay the cost of medical care to an injured party regardless of whether the policy-

79

holder is liable. Written in conjunction with general and personal liability policies. A similar coverage, AUTOMOBILE MEDICAL PAYMENTS, is available in automobile liability policies.

MEDICARE — The hospital insurance system and the supplementary medical insurance system created by the 1965 amendments to the Social Security Act.

MERCANTILE OPEN STOCK BURGLARY POLICY — See OPEN STOCK BURGLARY POLICY.

MERCANTILE REPORT — See INSPECTION and CREDIT REPORT.

MERCANTILE RISK — A property location used for the selling of merchandise, as distinguished from a habitational risk or a manufacturing risk in which goods are processed.

MERCHANDISE — Goods for sale.

MERIT RATING — A system of rating in which the experience of the individual risk is a factor in determining the rate.

MESSENGER AND INTERIOR ROBBERY INSURANCE — Insures the owner of money, securities and other property against loss by robbery inside the premises and from a messenger outside the premises. Often called inside and outside hold-up.

MILL CONSTRUCTION — Before the regular use of steel or concrete in building construction, many brick manufacturing buildings were built with floor and wall construction of an unusually heavy timber. This type of building is frequently found in the cotton and woolen mills of New England. It came, therefore, to be called "mill" construction. It is considered to be superior in fire-resistive qualities to ordinary brick or masonry construction with wood joists.

MINIMUM PREMIUM — The lowest flat or earned policy charge for which a policy will be issued or for which coverage will be provided.

MISREPRESENTATION — Misleading the company as to material facts affecting a policy or the settlement of a loss, either by directly or indirectly lying. Misrepresentation as to material facts voids policies.

MOBILE HOME INSURANCE — A special policy has been designed to meet the needs of mobile home owners or occupants, covering physical damage to the home, contents and personal liability while the home is used as a permanent residence.

MODEL BILL — Proposed legislation from a national organization for use by states choosing to do so.

MONEY AND SECURITIES BROAD FORM POLICY — Insures a business against "ALL RISKS" of loss or destruction of money and securities other than employee dishonesty and forgery. Applies both inside and outside the policyholder's premises. Also covers loss of other property and damage to the premises by safe burglary and robbery.

MONITORING COMPETITION — Measuring the degree of economic rivalry or striving among sellers of insurance within a market for a given type of insurance.

MONOPOLISTIC STATE FUND — A state-controlled workers compensation plan which writes insurance on such risks within the state and prohibits private insurers from doing so.

MORAL HAZARD — A condition or characteristic by which an insured intends to profit from an insured loss.

MORALE HAZARD — The condition which exists when an insured becomes lax in matters of safety and fire prevention because insurance is in force to pay for a loss which may occur.

MORBIDITY TABLE — A listing of data showing the accident or sickness rates of persons at each age.

MORTGAGE CLAUSE — Same as MORTGAGEE CLAUSE.

MORTGAGE (or MORTGAGEE) CLAUSE — Language attachable to an insurance policy covering mortgaged property which affords the mortgagee certain rights (e.g., that loss payments shall be payable to mortgagor and mortgagee as their interests may appear, that the mortgagee's right of recovery from the insurer shall not be adversely affected by any act or failure to act by the mortgagee, etc.).

MOTEL-HOTEL PROGRAM — A package policy combining the various coverages applicable to the operation of motels, hotels and similar establishments. Basically it covers fire and allied lines, liability, burglary and robbery insurance, and sometimes it includes fidelity insurance for employees. See SPECIAL MULTI-PERIL POLICY.

MOTOR TRUCK CARGO (CARRIERS FORM) — This inland marine form indemnifies an owner or operator of a motor truck, on which is carried property of others, against what the owner or operator may become liable to pay to the owners of the property carried as the result of loss or damage occurring while transporting the property. The Interstate Commerce Commission, as well as many state laws, requires a common carrier to have such insurance before being licensed. See MOTOR TRUCK CARGO (OWNERS FORM).

MOTOR TRUCK CARGO (OWNERS FORM) — Insures the owner of a truck against loss to owned property while being transported. See MOTOR TRUCK CARGO (CARRIERS FORM).

MOTOR VEHICLE ACCIDENT INDEMNIFICATION CORPORATION (NEW YORK) — This corporation exists to pay certain claims of innocent victims of New York motor vehicle accidents caused by uninsured motorists, where the victim is not an insured under family protection coverage.

MULTI-COVERAGE ACCOUNT PLAN (MAP) — A program providing favorable rate treatment for large risks written on an account basis. The plan applies to a combination of property and liability policies written by one insurer for one insured and having common expiration or anniversary dates. Not to be confused with the INDIVIDUAL RISK PREMIUM MODIFICATION PLAN, which relates to package policies of the Special Multi-Peril program. Lower rates are developed in the MAP program based on risk and expense modification and also the use of deductibles.

MULTI-LINE INSURANCE — See MULTI-PERIL INSURANCE.

MULTI-PERIL INSURANCE — Synonymous with multi-line insurance, a policy including both property and casualty coverage (e.g., a homeowners policy).

MULTIPLE LOCATION POLICY — A policy covering real or personal property subject to a single common interest (owner, tenant, or one holding a financial interest or title) at a number of different locations. Such policies are rated under a special plan.

MUSICAL INSTRUMENT FLOATER — An inland marine form designed to insure musical instruments against many different kinds of loss or damage.

MUTUAL ATOMIC ENERGY REINSURANCE POOL — A pool formed by mutual casualty and fire companies to provide bodily injury and property damage insurance for private nuclear reactor installations. Similar to stock company syndicate, AMERICAN NUCLEAR INSURERS.

MUTUAL INSURANCE — Protection written by an incorporated insurer having no capital stock and directed by policyholders who are its owners. As an operating cushion for solvency, mutual insurers are required by law to maintain surplus funds. Such surplus funds parallel the capital and surplus funds required by capital stock insurers as margins for solvency. See CAPITAL STOCK INSURANCE.

MYSTERIOUS DISAPPEARANCE — The vanishing of insured property in an unexplained manner. Previously there were disputes under theft policies as to whether property mysteriously lost had or

NATIONAL COMMITTEE ON INSURANCE GUARANTY FUNDS (NCIGF) — An insurance industry committee organized to assist state property and casualty guaranty associations. The committee consists of 12 members, three each from the three major company trade associations (American Insurance Association, National Association of Independent Insurers, and Alliance of American Insurers) and three from independent companies. The headquarters, currently at AIA, rotate between the three associations. See GUARANTY FUND.

NATIONAL COUNCIL ON COMPENSATION INSURANCE — An association of insurance companies providing workers compensation insurance. Main functions: rate making, collecting related statistics, and developing rating plans relative to compensation insurance. Operates through administrative bureaus located in many states. Headquarters, New York.

NATIONAL FIRE PROTECTION ASSOCIATION — An organization of those interested in the prevention of damage by fire. Its membership includes insurance companies, rating bureaus, manufacturers of fire prevention and extinguishing equipment, and officers of corporations in charge of fire prevention and safety work on land and at sea. Sets standards and issues constructive literature on the subject. Headquarters, Boston.

NATIONAL FLOOD INSURANCE ACT OF 1968 — An act establishing a basis for flood insurance as a joint venture between the private insurance industry and the federal government. The federal government has since taken over the entire program.

NATIONAL SAFETY COUNCIL — An association chartered by Congress to carry out a national program for reducing accidents of all kinds. The Council disseminates information on accident prevention; offers a public information and publicity program for newspapers, radio, television, etc.; cooperates with public officials at federal, state and local levels; and, in general, provides national leadership in the field of safety. Headquarters, Chicago.

NATIONAL WORKERS COMPENSATION REINSURANCE POOL — A reinsurance organization in which hazardous workers compensation risks assigned to insurers under various insurance plans are reinsured into a pool in which all companies participate proportionately, distributing losses so that undue loss to any one company may be avoided. At this time the Pool operates in 30 states. Headquarters, New York.

NATIONWIDE INTER-COMPANY ARBITRATION AGREEMENT — An arrangement whereby insurance companies settle automobile physical damage subrogation issues between themselves without the delays and expenses of litigation. All companies subject to this agreement bind themselves to submit disputed subrogation claims against another signatory company. Disputes are settled by local arbitration committees from a study of the claim files, usually without the need to call witnesses. The agreement is administered by the Insurance Arbitration Forum, headquartered in New York.

NATIONWIDE MARINE DEFINITION — The 1953 NAIC recommendations, since adopted by most states, of those subjects which should be considered as marine insurance for regulatory purposes: insurance covering domestic shipments being transported or subject to transportation, insurance on instrumentalities of transportation and communication, and property floaters covering property being transported or subject to being transported. While the Definition does not differentiate between ocean and inland marine insurance, its scope is primarily inland.

NEGATIVE FILM INSURANCE — Pays a producer of commercial films the cost of reshooting should the film suffer damage in the course of production.

NEGLIGENCE — The failure to exercise the care that an ordinary prudent person would exercise: either doing that which a prudent person would not do, or failing to do that which a prudent person would do.

NET LINE — The amount of insurance the company carries on a risk after deducting reinsurance from its "gross" line. See NET RETENTION and RETENTION.

NET PREMIUM — 1) The gross (paid) premium less any return premium or dividend. 2) The premium less the commission.

NET PROFIT — 1) In accounting, the difference between all income and all outgo, including reserves provided for expected outgo. 2) A subject of insurance if a loss of net profit is caused by an insurable peril.

NET RETENTION — The amount for which a company is liable for its own account, i.e., its gross amount less any reinsurance it may have secured. See NET LINE and RETENTION.

NEW FOR OLD — An expression in Marine insurance which means that when repairs are made, new parts or equipment are supplied in place of old ones that have been lost or damaged. An insurance policy may stipulate that the difference between the old and new costs are either excluded or included in its coverage.

NEW YORK BOARD OF FIRE UNDERWRITERS — An organization of companies operating in New York State. This body supervises loss adjustments and adjusters, carries on the inspection of electrical wiring throughout the state, operates the New York City salvage corps, and interests itself in the welfare of the business in the state.

NEW YORK INSURANCE EXCHANGE — A newly formed (1980) property-liability underwriting exchange patterned after the syndicate type of operation of LLOYD'S OF LONDON. The chief differences the Exchange has with Lloyd's are that the New York Exchange permits corporate as well as individual members, and their liability is limited to the amount of funds invested.

NO-FAULT AUTOMOBILE INSURANCE — Coverage designed to compensate victims of automobile accidents without the necessity of proving negligence on anyone's part. No-fault laws passed by different states vary greatly in their scope and application. Most provide that a victim's own insurance will allow a victim to sue in tort, once expenses or injuries have passed a stipulated threshhold (monetary or otherwise).

NONADMITTED ASSETS — Those assets of an insurance company which under state insurance laws or regulations are not recognized as assets for statutory reporting purposes, e.g., premiums uncollected over 90 days old, furniture and fixtures, etc. See ADMITTED ASSETS.

NONADMITTED INSURANCE — Protection written by an insurer on a risk located in a state in which the insurer is not licensed. Such an insurer is referred to as a nonadmitted insurer.

NONASSESSABLE POLICY — Insurance coverage in which the policyholder cannot be required to contribute in the event the insurer becomes unable to pay its losses. The large majority of policies in force in this country are nonassessable. Moreover, GUARANTY FUNDS exist in most states to cover insolvency losses. See ASSESSABLE INSURANCE.

NONCANCELLABLE — A provision in some policies (crop-hail insurance, ocean marine insurance, health insurance) that neither policyholder nor insurer may terminate the contract during its term.

NONCURRENT — The condition existing when two or more policies on a risk do not cover identically (a condition to be avoided because of difficulty in adjusting as well as the possibility that the insured will recover less than anticipated).

NONFORFEITURE VALUE — A benefit to a life insurance policyholder which provides the amount of money (CASH SURRENDER VALUE), the amount of extended term insurance, or the amount of paid-up insurance available from a life insurance policy to its owner when terminated by that person before the policy matures.

NONOWNER AUTOMOBILE LIABILITY INSURANCE — Coverage for the policyholder against liability incurred while driving an automobile not owned or hired by the policyholder or resulting from the use of someone else's automobile on the insured's behalf, e.g., an employee using a personal car for the employer's business purpose. This coverage is automatically included in personal (and most commercial) automobile policies.

NONPARTICIPATING INSURANCE — Policies which do not share in any policyholder dividends declared by the company. See PARTICIPATING INSURANCE.

NONRECORDING CHATTEL MORTGAGE POLICY — An insurance contract protecting a lender (usually a bank or small loan company) from loss arising from not having recorded a mortgage given as security for a loan. With such a policy, time and expense to record numerous mortgages are avoided.

NONWAIVER AGREEMENT — A signed agreement in which the insured stipulates that the continuance of a loss adjustment process by the insurer shall not be construed as an admission of liability by the insurer. Used when there are substantial questions as to the amount of the claim or whether the policy affords coverage at all.

NUCLEAR ENERGY LIABILITY—PROPERTY INSURANCE ASSOCIATION (NEW-PIA) — Former name of AMERICAN NUCLEAR INSURERS.

NURSING HOME PROFESSIONAL LIABILITY POLICY — Protects a nursing home against claims for injury resulting from negligence of the nursing home staff.

O

OBLIGEE — The party in whose favor a bond runs, i.e., the party protected from loss under the bond.

OBLIGOR — One bound by the obligation covered by a bond, also called the principal.

OCCUPANCY — 1) The use to which a building is put. 2) The type of contents a building contains.

OCCUPATIONAL DISEASE — Impairment of health due to continuous exposure to hazards inherent in a person's occupation. Compensable under most workers compensation laws.

OCCUPATIONAL SAFETY AND HEALTH ACT OF 1970 (OSHA) — A Federal statute establishing requirements for safe and healthy working conditions on a nationwide basis. Enforced by Labor Department safety inspectors and providing compilation of relevant statistics on work injuries and illnesses.

OCCURRENCE — 1) In a non-insurance sense, an incident, event or happening. In insurance, the term may be defined as continual, gradual or repeated exposure to an adverse condition which is neither intended nor expected to result in injury or damage, as contrasted with an accident, which is a sudden happening. In reinsurance, *per occurrence* coverage permits all losses arising out of one event to be aggregated instead of being handled on a risk-by-risk basis. 2) One basis or determinant for calculating the amount of loss or liability in insurance or reinsurance when an aggregation of related losses is to constitute a single subject of recovery. For example, in property catastrophe reinsurance treaties, occurrence is usually defined so that all losses within a specified period of time involving a particular peril are deemed an occurrence.

OCEAN MARINE INSURANCE — The protection of ships, their cargoes, and the freight, including protection and indemnity insurance to cover shipowner liabilities for loss of life to any person, illness or injury to crew, damage to cargoes carried, and damages to fixed or floating objects.

OFF PREMISES CLAUSE — Language which may be added to a policy indicating that personal property is covered when elsewhere than on the premises described in the policy.

OFFICE BURGLARY AND ROBBERY POLICY — A policy covering loss of money, securities, office equipment and fixtures by robbery (inside or outside) and burglary.

OFFICE PACKAGE POLICY — See SPECIAL MULTI-PERIL POLICY.

OFFICERS AND DIRECTORS LIABILITY INSURANCE — See DIRECTORS AND OFFICERS LIABILITY INSURANCE.

OMNIBUS CLAUSE — A part of an automobile or yacht liability policy which extends coverage to persons and organizations other than the named insured, such as members of the insured's family, servants and others using the automobile with the owner's permission. When these extensions were introduced, the policy was said to have an "omnibus clause."

OPEN ENROLLMENT — A period of time during which new subscribers may elect to enroll in a health insurance plan or prepaid group practice. In the Health Maintenance Organization Act of 1973 (P. L. 93-222), the term refers to periodic opportunities for the general public, on a first-come, first-served basis, to join an HMO.

OPEN POLICY — An insurance contract designed to cover shipments fluctuating in number and value with varying amounts of insurance, requiring the insured to report periodically to the insurer details of those shipments. An initial deposit premium is required at the inception of the policy, with premiums due calculated after the reports are received by the insurer. The open policy does not specify an expiration date, which is another feature of its open and continuous nature. Ocean marine cargo policies are generally written on this basis. See REPORTING POLICY.

OPEN STOCK BURGLARY POLICY — A coverage of merchandise, furniture, fixtures, and equipment against loss by burglary or robbery of a watchman while the premises are not open for business, including damages to the premises.

OTHER INSURANCE CLAUSE — Language in many policies which states the method for apportioning the loss between two or more policies covering the same property at the time of loss.

OUTBOARD MOTOR AND BOAT POLICY — A class of inland marine business covering boats, motors, and equipment for named perils (fire, collision, and theft) or, at a higher premium, for "all risks." Some policies include liability cover for property damage to other vessels.

OUTSERVANT — In workers compensation, insurance written to protect a domestic servant whose principal duties are outside, such as a gardener or chauffeur.

OUTSIDE EMPLOYEE — An employee such as a salesperson, messenger, or inspector whose duties keep the employee away from headquarters. Frequently used in bonding.

OUTSIDE HOLDUP INSURANCE — Messenger robbery insurance.

OVERINSURANCE — Coverage in amounts greater than the value of the property insured or the amount of loss sustainable by the insured (e.g., several policies of hospitalization insurance for a total amount in excess of daily room charges).

OVERLAPPING INSURANCE — When two or more different kinds of policies cover the same loss, the insurance is said to be "overlapping," as opposed to two or more policies of the same kind, which is "contributing" insurance. Contributing insurance is illustrated by two fire insurance policies covering the same loss. However, if an inland marine policy and a fire policy cover the same loss, they are overlapping insurance. See CONTRIBUTION CLAUSE and GUIDING PRINCIPLES.

OVERRIDING COMMISSION — That portion of a commission received and retained by a general agent after paying the other portion to a producing agent whose business is supervised by that general agent. Also known as overwriting commission.

OWNERS AND CONTRACTORS PROTECTIVE LIABILITY IN-SURANCE — Insures the legal liability of contractors and others for the negligent acts of independent contractors engaged by them and also, in some cases, for their own negligent supervision of the work performed.

OWNERS' EQUITY — 1) The interest of owners in an enterprise. 2) The excess of assets over liabilities of an enterprise.

OWNERS, LANDLORDS AND TENANTS LIABILITY INSUR-ANCE (OL&T) — Insurance of the liability arising from the ownership, occupancy, operation or maintenance of premises.

OWNERSHIP OF EXPIRATIONS — In the operation of the AMERICAN AGENCY SYSTEM, the independent agent's right to have or hold as property the records of customers secured and served by that agent (dates and details of expiring policies). Such ownership is contrasted with an EXCLUSIVE AGENT'S records of policyholders served by the exclusive agent which are owned by the insurer represented by the exclusive agent.

P

P AND I INSURANCE — Protection and indemnity insurance for shipowners, contractors, and charterers against liabilities arising out of the operation of the vessel for loss of life to any person, illness or injury to passengers and crew, damage to cargo while loading, carrying or unloading cargo, damage to piers and docks, and removal of wreckage as required by law.

PACKAGE POLICY — A combination of property-liability coverages of two or more separate policies in one contract with one premium. The development of package policies is a move toward economy and efficiency in giving the policyholder one document instead of several.

PAIR-AND-SET CLAUSE — An inland marine policy provision which requires the insurer, at the insured's option, to restore or pay for the entire pair or set of jewelry or fine arts when only a part has been lost, destroyed, or damaged.

PARAPET — A division wall or fire wall which, if it is to be accepted as a standard division, must extend through the roof and usually several feet above it. It (if brick or concrete) is usually topped with tile. The part above the roof is the "parapet."

PARCEL POST INSURANCE — An inland marine form that insures against the loss of merchandise in transit by government parcel post.

PARENT COMPANY — The organization which owns or controls one or more subsidiaries.

PARTIAL DISABILITY — Usually defined as inability caused by a covered illness to perform one or more of the functions of one's regular job. See TOTAL DISABILITY and PERMANENT AND TOTAL DISABILITY.

PARTIAL LOSS — Is one involving less than all of the values insured or calling on the policy to pay less than its maximum amounts.

PARTICIPATE — To share in the writing of a risk, the ASSUMPTION OF LIABILITY.

PARTICIPATING INSURANCE — A designated class of insurance which shares in the dividends declared by the company to policyholders. While mutual insurers issue participating policies mostly, and stock insurers usually issue nonparticipating policies, either type of insurer may seek authorization from its domiciliary state insurance department to issue the other type of policy. See DIVIDEND.

PARTICULAR AVERAGE — In ocean marine insurance, a loss (partial or total) which falls on one or more property(ies) or interest(s) being shipped, as opposed to a GENERAL AVERAGE.

PARTY WALL — A wall separating two buildings but common to both.

PAUL VS. VIRGINIA — A famous lawsuit decided in 1869 by the U.S. Supreme Court, in which the court held that insurance was not commerce and therefore not interstate commerce. Thus, insurance was not subject to Federal control. This was upset by the Supreme Court in 1944 in an equally famous case brought against the Southeastern Underwriters Association, usually referred to as the S.E.U.A. case. The citation is Paul vs. Virginia, 8 Wall. 168, 19 L. Ed. 35T (1868).

PAYMASTER ROBBERY INSURANCE — Insurance of payroll monies against loss by robbery inside or outside the insured's premises. The broad form policy covers payroll funds against "all risks" of loss or damage.

PAYMENT BOND — A bond given by a principal, usually a contractor, to guarantee payment for labor or materials used in the work under a contract.

PAYROLL AUDIT — An examination and verification of a policyholder's records of employees entitled to compensation, and the amounts expended therefor, which is used in determining the premium for certain lines of insurance such as workers compensation. The company sends out "payroll auditors" to determine the accuracy of the policyholder's figures. See AUDITOR.

PENALTY OF THE BOND — In a surety bond, the amount guaranteed or the limit of the company's liability.

PENSION TRUST LIABILITY INSURANCE — See FIDUCIARY LIABILITY INSURANCE.

PER DIEM BUSINESS INTERRUPTION INSURANCE — Coverage which provides that the amount recoverable is limited to a fixed amount per day or part thereof in which the manufacture of goods is prevented by an insured loss.

PERFORMANCE BOND — See CONTRACT BOND.

PERIL — The cause of loss (e.g., fire, explosion, accident).

PERILS OF THE SEA — Causes of loss unique to the operation of ships and their cargoes, i.e., sinking, stranding, heavy weather, etc., but not fire, lightning or theft.

PERMANENT AND TOTAL DISABILITY — Inability to perform one's own (and sometimes, any) occupation which lasts for a stated period of time and is caused by a covered illness or injury. See PARTIAL DISABILITY and TOTAL DISABILITY.

PERPETUAL INSURANCE — A form of insurance (principally fire) written without expiration date. Originated in Philadelphia and largely confined to that city and its surroundings, the policyholder makes a deposit with the insurance company, and the interest earnings from the funds so collected pay the losses suffered.

PERSONAL ACCIDENT INSURANCE — Protection of an individual against loss caused by accident.

PERSONAL ARTICLES FLOATER — Worldwide coverage on an "all-risk" basis for scheduled, valuable personal property.

PERSONAL AUTO POLICY — Coverage designed to replace both the family auto policy and the special package auto policy as the "standard" form for insuring private passenger autos and certain types of nonbusiness trucks.

PERSONAL EFFECTS FLOATER — An inland marine policy which insures articles (usually accompanying travelers) against "all-risks" while away from home.

PERSONAL INJURY PROTECTION (PIP) — Also known as no-fault insurance, providing insurance for medical costs, loss of earnings, additional living expenses, and funeral costs for occupants of the insured automobile and pedestrians other than those insured under other policies. See NO-FAULT AUTOMOBILE INSURANCE.

PERSONAL LINES — Types of insurance written for individuals rather than businesses (for which the term COMMERCIAL LINES applies).

PERSONAL PROPERTY — Property other than REAL PROPERTY: chattels.

PERSONAL PROPERTY FLOATER (PPF) — A broad form of inland marine policy issued to householders, insuring all furniture and household effects, wherever they may be, on an "all-risk" basis.

PERSONAL SURETY — Surety furnished by an individual, as distinguished from surety furnished by a surety company, called a "corporate surety." See SURETY.

PERSONAL THEFT INSURANCE — Coverage of personal property and household goods against loss by theft in and out of residential premises. Issued in the ordinary form and in a broad form, the latter including mysterious disappearance and certain more liberal provisions.

PHARMACISTS PROFESSIONAL LIABILITY INSURANCE — Protects pharmacists and their professional staff against claims for personal injury arising from malpractice, error or mistake in the performance of their professional services.

PHYSICAL HAZARD — Danger of loss or liability arising from the condition, occupancy, or use of property, as opposed to such danger arising from the character of the policyholder. See MORAL HAZARD and MORALE HAZARD.

PHYSICIANS AND SURGEONS PROFESSIONAL LIABILITY INSURANCE — Protects physicians and surgeons against claims for personal injury arising from malpractice, errors or mistakes in rendering professional services. At this time a most expensive coverage due to high jury awards against the medical profession.

PILFERAGE — Theft in small quantities, i.e., not limited to the taking of a whole package or all of the property insured.

PIRACY — Robbery on the high seas, typically the seizure of a vessel and cargo.

PLACER — The person in an insurance broker's office who directly negotiates with insurance companies for the acceptance or rejection of business.

PLATE GLASS INSURANCE — See GLASS INSURANCE.

POLICY — The formal written contract of insurance.

POLICY FEE — A charge made by an agent on small premium policies, in addition to the premium set forth in the policy, which is kept by the agent. The practice is made illegal under the insurance laws of most states.

POLICY PROOF OF INTEREST, FULL INTEREST ADMITTED — In marine insurance, a provision whereby the insurer agrees not to deny coverage for lack of insurable interest. This creates an honorable rather than legally enforceable agreement.

POLICY WRITING AGENT — An agent who has been extended the authority to prepare policies.

POLICY YEAR — The year commencing with the effective date of a policy or with the renewal date of that policy, to be distinguished from calendar year, which always starts from January 1. A term of particular importance in the collection of loss statistics.

POLICY YEAR EXPERIENCE — See ACCIDENT YEAR EXPERIENCE.

POLICYHOLDER — The party to whom a policy is issued, and who pays a premium to an insurer in consideration of the latter's promise to provide insurance protection.

POLICYHOLDER SURPLUS — See SURPLUS TO POLICYHOLDERS.

POOL — A joint insurance or underwriting operation in which the participant insurers assume a predetermined interest in all business written. Pools are managed by professionals with expertise in the classes of business undertaken. The members share proportionately in the premiums, losses, expenses and profits. An "association" or a "syndicate" is synonymous with a pool.

PORT — A place in which goods are sent out of a country or are received from abroad. The location of customs officials will usually determine what is called a port.

PORTFOLIO — A defined body of a.) insurance (policies) in force (a premium portfolio), b.) outstanding losses (a loss portfolio), or c.) company investments (an investment portfolio).

POSITION SCHEDULE BOND — A bond which guarantees the honesty of those holding named positions in a firm, as opposed to a bond which refers to named individuals.

POST INDICATOR VALVE (PIV) — When water mains are buried around industrial plants protected by automatic sprinklers, the flow of water in a buried pipe may be controlled by a valve which projects above the ground and has an indicator showing whether it is open or closed. Such valves are post indicator valves, abbreviated on diagrams as "P.I.V."

POWER OF ATTORNEY — A document which authorizes a person to act for another within the limitations it contains. A subscriber to

95

an interinsurance exchange executes such a document in favor of the person who operates the exchange.

POWER PLANT INSURANCE — Formerly used as a substitute title for BOILER AND MACHINERY INSURANCE.

PRE-EXISTING CONDITION — Injuries from accidents which occur earlier than, and sicknesses which begin earlier than, the date on which insurance becomes effective. Individual health insurance policies (and some group policies) generally cover only injuries from accidents which occur after the individual's coverage becomes effective, and only sicknesses which begin (or are first manifested) after the individual's coverage has been in effect for a period of time (often 15 days).

PREFERRED RISK — The subject matter of an insurance policy considered to be particularly desirable.

PREMISES — The building (or section of a building) insured or containing the insured property. Depending on policy conditions, it may also include an adjacent area.

PREMIUM — The amount of money an insurance company charges to provide coverage.

PREMIUM DISCOUNT — A percentage reduction based upon the size of the premium. Justification for this is that the proportionate cost for issuing and servicing a policy often becomes less as the premium increases. Not available in all states.

PREMIUM AND DISPERSION CREDIT PLAN — A plan for large commercial fire insurance accounts (with two or more locations) providing premium credits for a.) size of premium, to reflect savings in expenses in handling a substantial account, and b.) number of locations and dispersion of values to reflect spread of risk.

PREMIUM EARNED — See EARNED PREMIUM and UNEARNED PREMIUM.

PREMIUMS IN FORCE — A figure in the standard form of the annual financial report of an insurance company, representing the initial premium on all policies which have not expired or been cancelled, i.e., which are still in force.

PREPAID LEGAL EXPENSE — See LEGAL EXPENSE INSURANCE.

PRESSURE VESSEL — Something designed to contain gas or vapor (such as steam) under pressure. A steam boiler is an excellent example.

PRINCIPAL — In suretyship, the principal is the one whose honesty, fidelity, or ability to perform is guaranteed.

PRINCIPAL SUM — The stated amount that a policy of health or accident insurance will pay in the event of a certain happening, such as accidental death, dismemberment, or loss of eyesight.

PRIORITY COMPANY — An insurer needing special regulatory attention as determined by a review of financial ratio reports produced under the NAIC INSURANCE REGULATORY INFORMATION SYSTEM.

PRIVATE PASSENGER CAR — An automobile primarily operated by the owner for personal use, as distinguished from commercial use, as with a truck or taxicab.

PROBABLE MAXIMUM LOSS (PML) — The anticipated maximum property fire loss that could result, given the normal functioning of protective features (firewalls, sprinklers, and a responsive fire department, among others), as opposed to MAXIMUM FORESEEABLE LOSS which is a similar valuation, but on a worst case basis with respect to the functioning of the protective features. Underwriting decisions would typically be influenced by PML evaluations, and the amount of reinsurance ceded on a risk would normally be predicated on the PML valuation. See MAXIMUM FORESEEABLE LOSS and MAXIMUM POSSIBLE LOSS.

PROCESSOR — As distinguished from a manufacturer, one who changes the condition of merchandise without changing its fundamental character (e.g., a dyer, a printer of patterns on fabric, or one who hardens metal parts for the owner).

PROCESSORS POLICY — An inland marine form which insures the property of a policyholder when it is on the premises of another for processing; e.g., dyeing, finishing, etc., and while in transit to and from the premises of the processor.

PRODUCER — The person who solicits insurance from the buyer and places it with the insurer. A broker, an agent, or a salaried solicitor.

PRODUCT LIABILITY — The liability which a merchant or a manufacturer may incur as the result of some defect in the product sold or manufactured.

PRODUCT RECALL INSURANCE — Pays the expense associated with government dictated recall of a product suspected of being defective and dangerous to consumers. Pharmaceutical, automobile and aircraft manufacturers are those mainly affected. This expense is not covered by the standard general liability policy.

PROFESSIONAL INSURANCE AGENTS (PIA) — Formerly National Association of Mutual Insurance Agents, a trade association whose purpose is to protect the business interests of its members, who also are members of state associations.

PROFESSIONAL REINSURER — A term used to designate an organization whose business is mainly reinsurance and related services, as contrasted with other insurance organizations which may operate reinsurance assuming departments in addition to their basic primary insurance business.

PROFIT-SHARING COMMISSION — See CONTINGENT COMMISSION.

PROFITS INSURANCE — Coverage for the loss of profit that the policyholder could have earned had the merchandise destroyed in a fire (or by a covered peril) been sold otherwise. A fire insurance policy on a stock of merchandise pays only for the value of damaged or destroyed merchandise, hence the need for profits insurance. Such insurance is generally provided by adding a SELLING PRICE CLAUSE to a policy covering stock. See SELLING PRICE CLAUSE.

PROHIBITED LIST — A list of those risks which a company is not willing to write.

PROHIBITED RISK — A risk which a company will not insure.

PROOF OF LOSS — A written statement of a claim giving the pertinent facts and data which may be in the form of an affidavit.

PROPERTY AND CASUALTY INSURANCE — Non-life insurance. Basically there is a broad insurance distinction between companies writing life and health insurance and those writing the property insurance or "non-life" lines of fire, marine, casualty, and surety. Numerous descriptive titles have been employed to describe this "non-life" area of operation. Although no one definition has yet been firmly established, some use the generic title "property and casualty" insurance, while others use "property and liability" insurance.

PROPERTY DAMAGE LIABILITY INSURANCE — A form of "third-party" protection covering the insured's legal liability for damage to property of others caused by the insured's negligence. See LIABILITY INSURANCE.

PROPERTY INSURANCE — "First-party" insurance of real and personal property against physical loss or damage, not to be confused with PROPERTY DAMAGE LIABILITY INSURANCE.

PROPERTY INSURANCE PLANS SERVICE OFFICE (PIPSO) — An advisory organization, formed in 1972, to provide technical and administrative services to state property (FAIR) plans and windstorm pools.

PROPOSAL — In life insurance (and to a limited extent in property-liability insurance), a written plan prepared by an agent or insurer proposing to a prospective insured that insurance be applied for; thus, the proposal is not an offer but rather is an invitation to negotiate in the form of a sales brochure.

PRO RATA CANCELLATION — Termination of a policy by the insurer, for which the return premium due the policyholder is the full proportionate part for the unexpired term. In other words, the pro rata refund is not a "short rate" return. See SHORT RATE CANCELLATION.

PRO RATA CLAUSE — See PRO RATA DISTRIBUTION CLAUSE.

PRO RATA DISTRIBUTION CLAUSE — A provision in a property policy which states that the insurance which has been written "blanket," i.e., one amount covering several items, shall be limited on each item to the proportionate amount which the value of the particular item bears to the total value of all insured items. See AVERAGE CLAUSE.

PROSPECT — One to whom insurance may be sold as a prospective purchaser or insured.

PROTECTION — 1) Water supplies and fire departments to fight fires. Real property is referred to as protected property when located in an area served by a public fire department. See TOWN GRADING. 2) The insurance afforded by a policy.

PROTECTION AND INDEMNITY INSURANCE — See P AND I INSURANCE.

PROTECTIVE LIABILITY INSURANCE — Insurance against claims which arise because of some secondary cause, such as the negligent act of some subcontractor engaged by a principal contractor or against an employer for the act of an employee.

PROTEST — The master's statement of the facts which gave rise to an accident as a part of the ocean marine proof of loss. The protest is so named, because the master is "protesting" that it was not the master's fault. See PROOF OF LOSS.

PROVISIONAL PREMIUM — See ADVANCE PREMIUM and DEPOSIT PREMIUM.

PROXIMATE CAUSE — That which brings about a result without the intervention of any other force. Important in insurance since it establishes which policy(ies) will pay for a loss; i.e., the one(s) insuring the peril which was the proximate cause of the loss.

PSYCHOLOGY OF ENTITLEMENT — See ENTITLEMENT, PSYCHOLOGY OF.

PUBLIC ADJUSTER — One who, for a fee, represents policyholders in the adjustment of their losses with insurance companies.

PUBLIC AND INSTITUTIONAL PROPERTY PLAN — Insurance against fire and allied perils specially designed for property such as hospitals, schools, churches, etc. Rates are reduced for fire prevention and fire safety programs by the insured and lower acquistion and handling expenses to the insurer.

PUBLIC LAW 15 — See McCARRAN-FERGUSON ACT.

PUBLIC LIABILITY INSURANCE — See LIABILITY INSURANCE.

PUNITIVE DAMAGES — Damages awarded separately and in addition to compensatory damages, usually on account of malicious or wanton misconduct, to serve as a punishment for the wrongdoer and, possibly, as a deterrent to others. Sometimes referred to as "exemplary damages" when intended to "make an example" of the wrongdoer.

PUP COMPANY — A subsidiary of a PARENT COMPANY.

PURE PREMIUM — 1) That part of the premium which is sufficient to pay losses and loss adjustment expenses only, but not other expenses. 2) The premium developed by dividing losses by exposure, disregarding any loading for commission, taxes, and expenses.

Q

QUOTA SHARE REINSURANCE — A form of pro rata reinsurance (proportional) in which the reinsurer assumes an agreed percentage of each insurance policy being insured and shares all premiums and losses accordingly with the reinsured.

R

RADIOACTIVE CONTAMINATION INSURANCE — Coverage against loss caused by radioactive contamination. Such coverage is excluded from most insurance contracts and is usually covered under policies issued by pools created for this purpose. Other risks which might occasionally be exposed to damage can obtain this insurance as an additional coverage to an existing policy. The endorsement may be used with a fire form and on inland marine insurance policies such as transit coverage for truckers or shippers.

RAILROAD INSURANCE RATING BUREAU (RIRB) — A rating bureau which rates railroad property and files with state insurance departments on behalf of its member companies and subscribers.

RAIN INSURANCE — Insurance against loss due to the fall of rain, which may result in reduced profits or earnings. Also available to vacationers, paying the insured amount if rain occurs on specific days.

RATE — The price for a unit of insurance; all units in a given policy, multiplied by the rate per unit, produce the premium. In fire insurance, the price per $100 of insurance for one year. The basis for pricing other types of insurance varies greatly—i.e., payroll is used in workers compensation insurance, area of retail floor space or sales volume is used in certain types of general liability insurance, etc.

RATE CARDS — Written records on file with rating bureaus showing the rate to be charged a risk following inspection or application of a schedule. See INSURANCE SERVICES OFFICE.

RATE FILING — A document, furnished to a state insurance department by an insurer or a rating bureau, providing detailed information on an insurance rate used or proposed. Some rate filings are made to inform insurance departments about rates already in use (in file-and-use states, or in use-and-file states), some are made in prior-approval states to seek the department's approval prior to using the rate.

RATING BUREAU — An association of insurers which: makes rates for the use of its affiliated insurers; devises territorial classifications, rating plans, schedules, manuals, policy forms, and building inspections; and performs related functions for companies. See ADVISORY ORGANIZATION.

REAL PROPERTY — The earth and all attached to it: land and buildings, also known as real estate.

REBATE — Anything of value given or promised a prospective insured or unlicensed party by an agent or broker as an inducement to purchase insurance, including part or all of the commission. Rebating is usually illegal for all parties involved.

RECIPROCAL EXCHANGE — See INTERINSURANCE EXCHANGE.

RECOVERY — Loss money which an insurance company gets back from reinsurance, salvage, or by subrogation against a third party at fault.

REDLINING — The designation by an insurer of a certain geographic area considered unacceptable for the writing of insurance,

101

usually illegal because it is considered to be UNFAIR DISCRIMINA-TION. Redlining is refusing to insure, refusing to renew, cancelling, charging a higher rate, or limiting the amount or type of property insurance solely because of the geographic location of a risk. Further, redlining involves risk selection criteria which are not based on sound underwriting and actuarial principles, reasonably related to actual or anticipated loss experience of risk(s) having similar characteristics. See UNFAIR DISCRIMINATION.

REDUCED RATE AVERAGE CLAUSE — Generally the same as COINSURANCE CLAUSE.

REFERENCE — In certain states, arbitration is called "reference." See ARBITRATION CLAUSE.

REGISTERED MAIL INSURANCE — An inland marine form which insures money and securities for banks and brokers while in transit by registered mail.

REGISTERED TONNAGE — The cargo capacity of commercial ships measured in "tons," figuring each ton to occupy 100 cubic feet.

REGULATION OF INSURANCE — Governmental control of the business of insurance by federal, state, or local law.

REINSTATEMENT — 1) Restoration of the amount of insurance depleted from a policy by payment of loss. Most fire policies contain an automatic reinstatement clause. 2) Reinstituting or putting coverage back into effect under a policy in which coverage has been suspended or cancelled for a part of the policy term.

REINSURANCE — 1) The transaction whereby an insurance company (the reinsurer), for a consideration, agrees to indemnify another insurance company known as the ceding company (the reinsured) against all or part of a loss which the latter may sustain under a policy or policies it has issued. 2) When referred to as "a reinsurance," the term means the relationship between reinsured(s) and reinsurer(s).

REINSURANCE ASSOCIATION OF AMERICA — A group of property-casualty professional reinsurers formed to undertake programs designed to create a national awareness of the role and function of the reinsurer to the public, governmental bodies and the insurance industry in general. Founded in 1968 with headquarters in Washington, D.C.

REINSURANCE TICKET — See TICKET, REINSURANCE.

REINSURANCE TREATY — See TREATY, REINSURANCE.

REINSURER — An organization which assumes the liability of an insurer by way of reinsurance.

RELEASE — A written acknowledgement that policy obligations have been fulfilled.

REMOVAL — The taking of property to some place other than at which it was insured. The standard fire insurance policy used in most states insures against damage done in removing the insured property from the path of the fire.

RENEWAL — A policy issued to replace one which has expired.

RENEWAL CERTIFICATE — A document issued by an insurance company to its policyholder indicating that the insurance policy to which the certificate refers is being renewed for another policy term.

RENT INSURANCE — Insurance which reimburses a building owner against loss of rental income if the building is not usable by a tenant because of some peril insured against.

RENTAL VALUE INSURANCE — Insurance which reimburses the owner-occupant of a building for the cost of renting some other place if the building is rendered unusable by some peril insured against.

REPLACEMENT COST INSURANCE — Protection which pays the cost to restore or replace damaged or destroyed property without deduction for depreciation. Automatically included in homeowners forms. See ACTUAL CASH VALUE.

REPORTING POLICY (OR FORM) — A policy in which the policyholder is required to report the values of a property insured to the company at certain intervals. A provisional premium is charged initially and the final premium is determined by applying the rate to the average of the values reported. See OPEN POLICY.

REPRESENTATION — Information communicated by the prospective insured to an insurer which will influence the latter's underwriting decision.

RESERVE — An amount representing a liability of an insurer. See UNEARNED PREMIUM RESERVE and LOSS RESERVE.

RESIDENCE EMPLOYEE — An employee whose duties are in and around the insured premises.

RESIDUAL MARKET MECHANISM — An arrangement (voluntary or required by law) among participating insurers in which applicants for a certain type of insurance who are unable to secure protection in the open market ("hard-to-place" risks) may be covered by such participating insurers.

RESPONDENTIA — The loaning of money on cargo being shipped overseas at a higher rate of interest than otherwise, the difference to compensate the lender for the provision that no repayment was expected if the voyage failed. If the loan were on the vessel, the arrangement was called BOTTOMRY. Thus, respondentia was an early form of cargo insurance, and BOTTOMRY was an early form of hull insurance.

RETAIL STORE POLICY — See SPECIAL MULTI-PERIL POLICY.

RETALIATORY LAWS — Laws, usually referring to taxes, which provide that State A will charge a citizen or a corporation of State B doing business in State A not less than State B would charge one of the citizens or corporations of State A doing business in State B.

RETENTION — 1) The amount which an insured or an insurer assumes as its own liability and which is not insured otherwise. 2) In reinsurance, the amount which a primary insurer assumes for its own account. In pro rata reinsurance contracts, the retention may be a percentage of the policy limit. In excess of loss contracts, the retention is a dollar amount of loss. See NET RETENTION.

RETENTION CLAUSE — A clause in a policy of reinsurance by which the ceding company agrees to retain for its own account a certain part of the line.

RETIRING FROM A LINE — The act of an insurer in cancelling an existing line or declining to renew it.

RETROACTIVE DATE — The earliest date for which coverage is afforded under a CLAIMS-MADE form. Usually the effective date of the first year of such policy form provided to the insured. See CLAIMS-MADE.

RETROCESSION — The transaction whereby a reinsurer cedes to another reinsurer all or part of the insurance it has assumed.

RETROSPECTIVE RATING — A plan under which the premium is determined after the policy has expired based on contractual factors, chiefly the loss experience of the insured during the policy term. Designed to encourage safety by the insured and to compensate the insurer if larger than expected losses are incurred.

RETURN COMMISSION — When a policy is cancelled, the company returns the unearned premium to the insured. An agent is under contractual obligation to refund the unearned portion of the commission and, as a matter of business practice, a broker does likewise.

RETURN FOR NO CLAIM — Certain policies, e.g., policies of marine insurance covering yachts, provide for a refund of part of the premium in the event that the policyholder makes no claim for loss during the term of the policy. In the standard yacht policy, such refund is usually 20%.

104

RETURN PREMIUM — That part of a premium returned to a policyholder—upon cancellation or partial cancellation of a policy, when rate adjustments are necessary, or when an advance premium is in excess of the actual premium.

REVERSE COMPETITION — An excess of economic rivalry among insurers for the services or influence of the intermediary in an insurance transaction (i.e., agent, broker, finance company, or bank), in comparison with such rivalry for choices being made by consumers. In normal markets with normal competition, sellers compete for services or influence of all intermediaries available, for which compensation is paid as a cost of production in the pursuit of consumer preferences. In such normal markets, the consumer faces competitive prices for goods and services offered, based on competitive costs of production. In other words, sellers strive among themselves for consumer preferences by offering the highest quality of goods and services at the lowest possible prices, which means their costs must be kept low. In markets having reverse competition, however, sellers compete more for services or influence of intermediaries than for the choices of consumers, since either the intermediaries "control" the market more by influencing consumer choices or else consumers exercise less preference than under normal market conditions. It then becomes advantageous for sellers to raise their compensation to intermediaries (which in turn increases their production costs), rather than compete for consumer preferences by offering the highest quality of goods and services at the lowest possible price. Other things equal, prices in markets having reverse competition are usually higher than they would be if reverse competition did not exist.

RIDER — Another word for ENDORSEMENT.

RIOT — Violent and tumultous actions by a number of people, coverage for which is included in the extended coverage endorsement.

RIOT AND CIVIL COMMOTION INSURANCE — Insurance against damage done by rioters or those engaged in civil commotion, included in the extended coverage endorsement to the standard fire policy. See CIVIL COMMOTION.

RISK — 1) Defined variously as uncertainty of loss, chance of loss, or the variance of actual from expected results. However defined, its existence is the reason people buy insurance. 2) The subject matter of an insurance contract, e.g., the building, cargo, or liability exposure insured.

RISK AND INSURANCE MANAGEMENT SOCIETY, INC. (RIMS) — Previously known as American Society of Insurance Management Inc. (ASIM), formed in 1950. A nonprofit association dedicated to the advancement of professional standards of risk management. RIMS sponsors educational programs and maintains relationships with insurers, brokers, rating organizations, regulatory and governmental bodies. Headquarters, New York.

ROBBERY — The taking of property by violence or threat of violence.

RUIN THEORY — A concept describing an insurer's vulnerability to insolvency, caused from too much growth in premium writings in relation to its policyholder surplus. Because an insurer must use its policyholder surplus (the difference between its assets and liabilities) to put new business on the books, the amount of its policyholder surplus is a limit to its growth. The ruin theory describes the threat of insolvency to an insurer at varying levels or projected growth in premium income.

RUNNING DOWN CLAUSE — The clause in an ocean marine hull policy which covers damage done to another ship by collision, and other property damage caused by collision.

S

SACRIFICE — In marine insurance, acts done for the welfare of all interests, such as the throwing overboard (jettison) of part of a cargo to keep the ship from sinking. See JETTISON and GENERAL AVERAGE.

SAFE BURGLARY INSURANCE — Protection against loss of property caused by forcible entry into a safe or vault. Damage to safes, vaults, and other property on the premises resulting from burglary is also covered unless caused by fire.

SAFE DEPOSIT BOX INSURANCE — Insurance against the loss of property contained in a safe deposit box.

SAFE DRIVER RATING PLAN — A merit rating program for private passenger cars whereby insureds with clean driving records qualify for lower automobile insurance premiums, and insureds who have an accident or moving traffic violation history pay higher premiums. The amount of premium is regulated by a point system, which assigns a certain number of points for accidents and traffic violations in which the insured is involved during a stated period, usually three years.

SAFETY ENGINEERING — See LOSS PREVENTION.

SAFETY RESPONSIBILITY LAWS — Another name for FINANCIAL RESPONSIBILITY LAWS.

SALESMANS SAMPLE FLOATER — An inland marine policy which insures valuable samples carried by salespersons.

SALVAGE — Property in a loss saved from further loss.

SALVAGE CORPS — Certain big cities have organizations similar to fire departments, the duties of which are limited to the prevention of damage to property during and after a fire rather than the extinguishing of the fire. Such organizations are maintained by the fire insurance companies and are called salvage corps.

SANBORN MAP — Maps of cities and towns giving details of construction and fire protection, made by the Sanborn Map Company. Formerly more common than today, fire insurers kept such map records in their offices to indicate the location and other details of their insured risks in order to prevent undue concentration in a given building, city block, or area. See MAP CLERK.

SCHEDULE — 1) The plan or formula applied to arrive at a fire insurance rate. 2) A list of insured properties, and the amount of insurance on each, which is attached to a "schedule" policy, as distinguished from a "blanket" policy. In the latter, one amount of insurance applies to the total of all insured properties. See SCHEDULE RATING.

SCHEDULE BOND — A fidelity bond covering a number of named individuals or positions (irrespective of who occupies them), as contrasted with a blanket bond, which covers all.

SCHEDULE RATING — A system of making fire insurance rates for commercial properties, determined by physical inspection of each risk. Such rates are made by modifying the class rates applying to a given classification—to the extent of the good or bad features of the individual risk, according to the schedule. For example, a certain commercial building may receive a credit because it is sprinklered, a debit because it is protected only by a volunteer fire department.

SCHEDULE POLICY — A listing of two or more items of property in a policy, with specified amounts of insurance applying to each item. On the other hand, if a policy were to provide one amount of insurance on several items of property, the policy would be known as a BLANKET POLICY.

SEASONAL RISK — An insured risk which is occupied only part of the year, such as a summer dwelling. In the case of a manufacturer, it may be a plant which is operated only a part of a year according to the season, such as a cannery.

SECURITY BOND — See SURETY BOND.

SELECTION — The process of accepting and rejecting risks in the attempt to produce a profit in underwriting. See CLASSIFICATION, DISCRIMINATION, and UNFAIR DISCRIMINATION.

SELF INSURANCE — The retention of sufficient exposure units by an entity to permit the operation of the LAW OF LARGE NUMBERS. Self insurance is a term often mistakenly used to describe the situation when an entity decides to retain its own risks. The mistake arises when the exposure units are too few in number to permit the application of the LAW OF LARGE NUMBERS. When the exposure units are too few, a better and less misleading term of such a practice is "self-assumption of risk."

SELLING AGENTS COMMISSION INSURANCE — Protection to indemnify an independent sales agent (sometimes known as a manufacturer's representative) for lost commissions on orders already received due to the inability of the manufacturer to produce the goods because of fire or other insured peril.

SELLING PRICE CLAUSE — An endorsement which can be added to a fire policy covering a stock of merchandise, which extends the policy to cover beyond the actual value of the stock. One form, covering only stock already sold, is available to both mercantile and manufacturing risks, and pays the price for which the stock had been sold. The other form, covering unsold stock, is available for manufacturers only and pays the price for which the owner expected to sell the stock. See PROFITS INSURANCE.

SETTLEMENT OPTION — The choice of payment method and frequency available to the beneficiary of a matured life insurance policy.

SETTLING AGENT — In marine insurance, a person authorized to pay losses out of funds provided by the marine underwriter. Such agents have broader powers than the claim agent, whose authority is limited to surveying and certification of losses.

S.E.U.A. CASE — See SOUTHEASTERN UNDERWRITERS ASSOCIATION.

SHOCK LOSS — A much larger loss than anticipated. Usually a loss large enough to have an impact on a company's underwriting results in any given territory. See PROBABLE MAXIMUM LOSS and MAXIMUM FORESEEABLE LOSS.

SHORT RATE CANCELLATION — Termination of a policy by the policyholder before its stated expiration, with the insurer refunding to the policyholder a return premium in less amount than the pro rata part that is still unearned to compensate the insurer for expenses incurred to that point, since the termination is at the request of the policyholder. See PRO RATA CANCELLATION.

SHORT TERM — A policy period of less than one year.

SICKNESS INSURANCE — A form of health insurance against loss by illness or disease.

SILVERWARE FLOATER — An inland marine form designed to insure silverware worldwide against all risks, usually by endorsement to a homeowners policy.

SINGLE INTEREST COVER (or INSURANCE) — Used in connection with property sold on the installment plan, it protects the lender of money advanced to purchase a property, but does not protect directly the borrower or purchaser.

SINKHOLE INSURANCE — Occurs notably in Florida, but found in other limestone areas, covering physical damage to dwellings and personal property caused directly by "sinkhole collapse." Sinkhole collapse is the sudden settlement or collapse of earth resulting from subterranean voids created by the action of water on limestone or similar rock formations. All licensed insurers writing property insurance in Florida were required at one time to join the Florida Sinkhole Reinsurance Association, which assumed all sinkhole policies written by members who shared through the Association equitably in the total premiums, losses, and expenses. After a five-year operation without a loss, the insurers in Florida were required to insure sinkholes under the extended coverage endorsement. The Association was then dissolved, although it was reborn shortly thereafter as the Florida Windstorm Association.

SLIP — A piece of paper submitted by a Lloyd's of London broker on which underwriters record their participation in a risk. In broader terms, it applies to any list of insurers or reinsurers providing the capacity for a risk.

SMOKE DAMAGE — Damage caused by smoke other than smoke which accompanies a hostile fire. One of the extended coverage endorsement perils, but subject to certain restrictions.

SMP — See SPECIAL MULTI-PERIL POLICY.

SNOWMOBILE INSURANCE — Covers snowmobiles against physical damage to the equipment, and legal liability for its use and operation.

SOCIAL INFLATION — The increased jury awards, increased liberal treatment of claims by workers compensation boards, legislated increases in benefit levels (in some cases retroactively), and new concepts of tort and negligence that emerge to increase insurance losses.

SOCIAL INSURANCE — Insurance provided by government.

SOCIETY OF ACTUARIES — An organization formed to promote actuarial and statistical knowledge applicable to life and health insurance. Headquarters, Chicago, Illinois. (Its property-liability insurance counterpart is the CASUALTY ACTUARIAL SOCIETY.)

SOCIETY OF CHARTERED PROPERTY & CASUALTY UNDER-WRITERS (CPCU) — Professional society of those who have been awarded the designation of Chartered Property Casualty Underwriter. (CPCU). Fosters research and continuing education of its members. Headquarters, Malvern, Pa.

SOCIETY OF INSURANCE ACCOUNTANTS (SIA) — An organization devoted to the discussion of accounting and statistical and management problems and the interchange of ideas with the objective of fostering the value of the accounting and statistical functions to the insurance industry. Headquarters, New York City.

SOCIETY OF INSURANCE RESEARCH — Stimulates research affecting all lines of insurance and fosters exchange on research methodology among Society members. Headquarters, Columbus, Ohio.

SOFTWARE — All documents, manuals, and written instructions which guide a computer operation. See HARDWARE.

SOUTHEASTERN UNDERWRITERS ASSOCIATION — The defendant in U.S. v. S.E.U.A., 322 U.S. 533 (1944), in which the Supreme Court held that insurance is commerce. Also known as the S.E.U.A. CASE. See INTERSTATE COMMERCE.

SPECIAL AGENT — A representative of an insurance company who travels a given territory dealing with agents and supervising the company's operations there. See STATE AGENT.

SPECIAL AUTOMOBILE POLICY — A combination private passenger Automobile policy designed to provide basic coverage at minimum cost. The lower premium is due to economies in acquisition and handling expenses, as well as reduced uniform coverage.

SPECIAL HAZARD — A hazardous risk or more generally a risk with manufacturing occupancy.

SPECIAL MULTI-PERIL POLICY — A package policy for commercial accounts containing four principal sections of coverage: property, liability, crime, and boiler and machinery. The basic policy contains declarations, general provisions and definitions applicable to these sections, and then the specific coverage requirements for each section are handled by separate forms. The types of accounts eligible for this policy can be grouped in eight categories: motel/hotel, apartment house, office, mercantile, service, industrial and processing, institution, and contractors.

SPECIFIC INSURANCE — A single amount of insurance covering a single type of insurable property, e.g., building or contents, used in contrast with BLANKET INSURANCE. Thus, a policy providing one amount of coverage on building and contents would be blanket insurance, whereas one providing a certain amount on the building and another amount on the contents would be specific insurance.

SPECIFIC RATE — A fire insurance rate which applies to SPECIFIC INSURANCE.

SPREAD LOSS REINSURANCE — A type of excess of loss property reinsurance which provides for a periodic adjustment of the reinsurance premium rate based on the reinsured's experience for preceding years (usually five) plus a loading for the purpose of compensating the reinsurer for: a) its expenses, b) the possibility of unusual losses, c) those losses occurring at the end of the period of the treaty, which the reinsurer might not have a chance to recoup if the treaty is not renewed, d) a catastrophe possibility, and e) the reinsurer's profit. In casualty reinsurance, adjustments to the above may be required for such other factors as economic and social inflation. Also known as CARPENTER PLAN.

SPRINKLER HEAD — A valve on an automatic sprinkler system which opens when subject to excessive heat from a fire, permitting water to flow in a circular fashion from overhead pipes, thus localizing the fire. See AUTOMATIC SPRINKLERS.

SPRINKLER LEAKAGE INSURANCE — Insurance against the damage done by the accidental discharge of water from automatic sprinklers and similar fire prevention devices.

STAMPING BUREAU — Same as AUDIT BUREAU.

STANDARD FORM — A form, a policy or other document used to write insurance, which has been adopted and is used by a large number of companies or has been promulgated by a rating bureau or legislature. The use of standard forms does away with much of the need to scrutinize every word of a policy form for meaning, since the standard has been examined and adjudicated by courts.

STANDARD POLICY — A policy generally in use and in some lines of insurance a policy prescribed by law. See STANDARD FORM.

STATE AGENT — A representative of an insurance company who travels a given territory (usually an entire state), dealing with agents and supervising the company's business with them. The state agent is usually senior to a special agent, whose territory is less than an entire state. See SPECIAL AGENT.

STATE ASSOCIATION OF INSURANCE AGENTS — In each state, insurance agents have formed organizations to discuss their problems and forward the best interests of the AMERICAN AGENCY

111

SYSTEM. Together these state associations make up the national INDEPENDENT INSURANCE AGENTS OF AMERICA or the PROFESSIONAL INSURANCE AGENTS. IIAA is mostly stock agents and PIA is mostly mutual, but both support the AMERICAN AGENCY SYSTEM.

STATEMENT OF VALUES — When a risk is rated with a blanket rate (i.e., when a single rate is to cover more than one item or building), the policyholder is asked to give the amount of value in each separate risk (and usually in the contents of each), so that a correct average may be determined. The information required is a "statement of values."

STATISTICAL AGENT — An organization authorized by the laws of most states to prepare the statistics required for the administration of rating laws. Company associations compiling statistics in a given state are subject to appointment by its individual commissioner.

STATUTE OF LIMITATIONS — A statute limiting the time within which a legal action may be brought.

STATUTORY ACCOUNTING PRINCIPLES (SAP) — Those principles required by state law which must be followed by insurance companies in submitting their financial statements to state insurance departments. Such principles differ from generally accepted accounting principles (GAAP) in some important respects, e.g., SAP requires that expenses must be recorded immediately and cannot be deferred to track with earned premiums. See GAAP.

STATUTORY UNDERWRITING PROFIT OR LOSS — See UNDERWRITING PROFIT OR LOSS.

STOCK — Merchandise for sale or in the process of manufacture, as distinguished from furniture, fixtures, or machinery.

STOCK INSURANCE — See CAPITAL STOCK INSURANCE.

STOP LOSS REINSURANCE — A company wishing to protect itself in the event its net loss ratio for a given year rises above a certain percentage may buy reinsurance which pays in excess of that figure up to a higher agreed percentage, beyond which the company is once more liable. In short, a plan which takes the sting out of an above-average net loss ratio.

STOREKEEPER BURGLARY AND ROBBERY POLICY — A package policy designed for small retail stores, insuring against losses from burglary or robbery. See BROAD FORM STOREKEEPERS POLICY.

STOREKEEPERS LIABILITY POLICY — A package policy designed for retail store operators, insuring against claims for bodily injury and property damage arising from their business operations. Excludes automobile liability.

STRANDING — Running aground, such as a vessel may do in shallow water.

SUB-AGENTS — Agents who sell insurance through other agents or through general agents.

SUBROGATION — In insurance, the substitution of one party (insurer) for another party (insured) to pursue any rights the insured may have against a third party liable for a loss paid by the insurer.

SUBSIDENCE — Damage due to land movement, e.g., a house on a hill may slide down the hill due to heavy rains. Not earthquake damage.

SUBSTANDARD RISKS — Risks which do not meet minimum underwriting criteria.

SUE AND LABOR CLAUSE — Language in marine and inland marine policies requiring the policyholder in event of loss to take all necessary means to save the property from further loss and recover from others who caused the loss. The insurer agrees to pay the costs, even if they exceed the policy's limit of liability.

SUNSET PROVISION — Language in a licensing statute or regulation stating that the licensing authority granted is for a specified period of time, and not until revoked as is customary.

SUPERINTENDENT OF INSURANCE — See COMMISSIONER OF INSURANCE.

SUPERSEDED SURETYSHIP RIDER — Fidelity losses often occur over a considerable period of time. Renewal or replacement of a fidelity bond includes this clause which states that the new bond pays all losses that would have been recoverable under the previous bond, except that the DISCOVERY PERIOD under that bond had expired. This provision would apply to any losses which occurred prior to the inception of the current bond.

SURETY — 1) The guarantee given for the fulfillment of an obligation. 2) The person or organization guaranteeing the fulfillment of an obligation. 3) The underwriter who guarantees something under a bond.

SURETY ASSOCIATION OF AMERICA — An organization of companies engaged in fidelity and surety bond underwriting, basically a form and rate-making body, but the organization also prepares manuals, collects and disseminates statistical data, provides a forum for the discussion of common problems of members, and engages in educational activities. Headquarters, New York.

SURETY BOND — A written agreement wherein one party (the surety) obligates itself to a second party (the obligee or beneficiary) to answer for the default of a third party (the principal) in failing to perform specified acts within a stated time. Such obligations include payment of debts and responsibility for defaults.

SURETYSHIP — The function of being a surety.

SURGEONS PROFESSIONAL LIABILITY INSURANCE — See PHYSICIANS AND SURGEONS PROFESSIONAL LIABILITY INSURANCE.

SURPLUS — The remainder after a company's liabilities are deducted from its assets.

SURPLUS LINE — 1) A risk or part thereof for which there is no available market in the ADMITTED MARKET. 2) All insurance written by nonadmitted insurers.

SURPLUS TO POLICYHOLDERS — As reported on a statutory basis, the sum of all unassigned surplus of a mutual insurer, or for a stock insurer, the sum of all unassigned surplus and capital.

SURVEY — The description of a subject of insurance made for the information of the insurer by an inspector or surveyor.

SURVEYOR — One who determines either the condition of insured marine property or the amount of loss or damage in ocean marine practice.

SYNDICATE — In insurance, usually a group of companies or underwriters who join together to insure property. See LLOYD'S SYNDICATE or HULL SYNDICATE and POOL.

SYNDICATE POLICY — A policy issued on behalf of a number of companies which share a risk or a class of risks. It lists the name of the participating companies and the liability assumed by each company, thus replacing a large number of policies, one from each company.

T

TAKE-ALL-COMERS — A proposal (or requirement in a few states) that an insurer must accept all applicants for a given type of insurance.

TAKEOVER DEFENSE INSURANCE — Protection to reimburse a corporation for expenses incurred (legal, investment advisory, communications, accounting, etc.) in successfully resisting an attempt to assume its ownership or control by a stock tender offer. Corporations eligible are those whose stock is either traded on public exchanges or is registered under Section 12 of the Securities Exchange Act of 1934.

TARGET (OR TARGET RISK) — 1) A risk which because of its large size or other characteristic must be offered to many insurers in order to be placed. Everybody "takes a shot at it." 2) Also, a large risk sought after by virtually all large brokers.

TARIFF — The rate made and published by a rating bureau. Also refers to the rules and schedules which are used to make the rates.

TENANTS POLICY — A form of homeowners policy sold to persons who rent their living quarters or are co-op apartment owners.

TEN-DAY EXAMINATION PERIOD — In health insurance, a notice on the first page of a policy that the policyholder has ten days in which to examine the policy and return it for full refund of premium if not satisfied. Often known as the "ten-day free look," the provision is now required in many states.

TENDER OFFER EXPENSE INSURANCE — See TAKEOVER DEFENSE INSURANCE.

TERM — The length of time for which a policy or bond is written.

TERM POLICY — A policy written for longer than one year. If for less than a year, it is a "short-term" policy.

TERM RATE — The insurance rate for a policy period longer than one year. If for less than a year, it is a "short-term" rate.

TERM RULE — The provision which stipulates the length of time for which a policy may be written and the discount, if any, applying to the rate or premium of policies issued for more than one year.

THEATRICAL FLOATER — An inland marine policy covering loss or damage to the scenery, costumes, and other properties of a theatrical production.

THEFT — A broad term meaning the wrongful taking of the property of another.

THIRD PARTY — The claimant under a liability policy, so called because the first two parties are the insured and insurer, who enter into the insurance contract which pays the third party's claim.

THIRD PARTY INSURANCE — Protection against liability to a third party. The first two parties are the insured and the insurer.

3-D POLICY — See COMPREHENSIVE DISHONESTY, DISAPPEARANCE AND DESTRUCTION POLICY.

TICKET, REINSURANCE — A notation in the form of a separate piece of paper attached to the daily report of an insurer, setting forth the details of reinsurance that has been effected.

TIME ELEMENT INSURANCE — See BUSINESS INTERRUPTION INSURANCE.

TITLE INSURANCE — Protection which indemnifies the purchaser of real estate against loss occasioned from defects in the legal title. A title insurance policy extends for the lifetime of the insured while owning the insured property. Largely written by insurers specializing in this class alone.

TORNADO — A destructive and whirling wind of extreme violence which is accompanied by a funnel-shaped cloud moving rapidly over land in a narrow path. The barometric pressure may drop so severely and rapidly that buildings actually explode from within.

TORNADO INSURANCE — See WINDSTORM INSURANCE.

TORT — A legal wrong arising from a breach of duty fixed by law, except under contract, causing injury to persons or property and redressible by legal action for damages.

TOTAL DISABILITY — Inability to perform any functions of any occupation, caused by a covered illness or injury. See PARTIAL DISABILITY and PERMANENT AND TOTAL DISABILITY.

TOTAL LOSS — 1) Loss of all the insured property. 2) Under a given policy, a loss involving the maximum amount for which that policy is liable.

TOURIST FLOATER — An inland marine form which insures the baggage and other possessions of a traveler or tourist.

TOWING CHARGES — An extension of an automobile physical damage policy which covers the cost of towing the insured car or providing emergency road service.

TOWN GRADING — See GRADING OF CITIES AND TOWNS.

TRACTOR/TRAILER — In insurance terms, not a farm tractor, but rather a motor truck type and the trailer to which it is attached.

TRADE ASSOCIATION — See ADVISORY ORGANIZATION.

TRANSPORTATION INSURANCE — Insurance of merchandise while being moved (e.g., cargo), while being subject to transportation (e.g., cargo in a warehouse), or while serving as an instrument of transportation and communication (e.g., bridges, tunnels, and television transmission towers). Usually the province of marine or inland marine underwriters.

TREATY, REINSURANCE — A reinsurance agreement between an insurance company and a reinsurer, usually for one year or longer, which may be divided into two broad classifications: a) the participating type which provides for sharing of risks between the ceding company and the reinsurer; and b) the excess type which provides for indemnity by the reinsurer only for loss which exceeds some specified predetermined amount.

TRIP INSURANCE — Insurance written to cover a single shipment of household furniture, personal effects, merchandise, and livestock against loss by specified perils or "all risks."

TRIP TRANSIT INSURANCE — See TRIP INSURANCE.

TRUCKERS LIABILITY — See MOTOR TRUCK CARGO.

TYPHOON — A hurricane-type storm originating in the Pacific Ocean, China Sea, and the Philippines.

U

UBERRIMAE FIDEI — Literally, of the utmost good faith. The basis of all insurance and reinsurance contracts. Both parties to the contract are bound to exercise good faith and do so by a full disclosure of all information material to the proposed contract.

ULTIMATE NET LOSS — In liability insurance, the amount an insured is obligated to pay because of settlement or adjudication.

UMBRELLA LIABILITY INSURANCE — A form of liability insurance protecting policyholders for claims in excess of the limits of their primary automobile, general liability, and workers compensation policies, and for some (few) claims excluded by their primary policies which are subject to a deductible, which may range from $250 for a personal umbrella to a minimum of $10,000 for a commercial umbrella.

UMPIRE — A person selected by two appraisers to help settle disputes in property insurance claims. If a company and a claimant fail to agree as to actual cash value or amount of loss, many policies provide that these be determined by appraisal. The appraisers appointed by the parties select an umpire. A decision of any two is binding.

UNAUTHORIZED INSURANCE — Insurance written by an insurer not licensed by the country or state in which the risk is located.

UNDERINSURANCE — Insurance which is insufficient in amount to cover a loss which the policyholder may suffer.

UNDERWRITER — One who accepts or rejects risks for an insurer (originally, by writing the person's name under the contract of insurance being issued).

UNDERWRITERS ADJUSTING COMPANY — A large company-owned adjustment bureau operating on a countrywide basis. Headquarters, Chicago.

UNDERWRITERS LABORATORIES, INC. (UL) — A nonprofit organization which maintains an extensive laboratory for testing the safety of electrical products and other devices, authorizing the use of the "UL" symbol on the device to indicate approval. Headquarters, Chicago.

UNDERWRITERS SALVAGE COMPANY OF CHICAGO — Appraises damaged, insured merchandise, including disposal, for the benefit of insurers. Headquarters, Elk Grove Village, Ill.

UNDERWRITERS SALVAGE COMPANY OF NEW YORK — Assists insurance companies in adjustment of losses through the reclamation, reconditioning and disposition of damaged merchandise. Headquarters, Clifton, New Jersey.

UNDERWRITERS SERVICE ASSOCIATION — A group of insurers banded together to write industrial risks on a pool basis, supplying the needed engineering service and inspections jointly. Similar to the Factory Insurance Association, but normally writing risks less highly protected than those in the F.I.A. Headquarters, Chicago.

UNDERWRITING — The process of selecting, classifying, evaluating, rating, and assuming risks.

UNDERWRITING PROFIT OR LOSS — 1) Money earned or lost by an insurer in its underwriting operations, as distinguished from money earned or lost in the investment of assets. 2) Earned premiums less losses, loss adjustment expenses incurred and other underwriting expenses incurred, usually determined monthly for managerial purposes.

UNEARNED PREMIUM — The portion of the premium representing the unexpired portion of the policy term.

UNEARNED PREMIUM RESERVE — The sum of all the premiums representing the unexpired portions of the policies which the insurer has on its books as of a certain date. It is usually calculated by a formula of averages of issue dates and the length of term. The reserve is equivalent to the amount of return premium due policyholders if the insurer should terminate the insurance. See EQUITY IN UNEARNED PREMIUM RESERVE.

UNFAIR DISCRIMINATION — Treating an applicant for insurance differently than other insureds because of any factor not related to the applicant's loss producing or expense producing qualities, e.g., charging a higher rate, among other possibilities, than the loss producing or expense producing qualities would justify. Factors such as a person's race, color, creed, or national origin that are unrelated to the chance of loss should not affect the writing of insurance. While making distinctions is essential in any insurance system to match individual risks with the rates appropriate for their class, unfair discrimination is illegal. See CLASSIFICATION and REDLINING.

UNIFORM FORMS — See STANDARD FORM.

UNINSURED MOTORIST COVERAGE — Under an auto policy, protection for the insured against bodily injury caused by the negligence of an uninsured or underinsured motorist.

UNITED STATES AIRCRAFT INSURANCE GROUP (USAIG) — A multi-company aviation pool writing a substantial volume of most types of aviation coverages, both domestic and international. Founded in 1928. Headquarters, New York.

UNIVERSAL MERCANTILE SCHEDULE — A method of making fire insurance rates which is the basis of many of the methods in use, particularly in the East.

UNOCCUPIED BUILDING — The temporary absence from a building of an occupant, but with the occupant's furniture and personal effects remaining, as opposed to a VACANT BUILDING, which has neither occupants nor contents.

UNSATISFIED JUDGMENT FUND — A state fund created to reimburse persons injured in automobile accidents who cannot collect damages awarded to them because the party responsible is either insolvent or uninsured. Such funds are often financed by an addition to the regular automobile registration fee and will only pay unsatisfied judgments up to fixed limits.

USE AND OCCUPANCY — See BUSINESS INTERRUPTION INSURANCE.

USUAL RANGES — The measurements within which key financial ratios of an insurance company may fluctuate and still pass the tests of the NAIC INSURANCE REGULATORY INFORMATION SYSTEM.

V

VACANT BUILDING — A building with nothing in it. If the furniture is in the building and the owner intends to return, the building is UNOCCUPIED.

VALUED POLICY — A policy in which the company agrees that the property insured is worth the amount of insurance, and therefore in the event of total loss pays the face value of the policy without need for proof of the value at that time.

VALUED POLICY LAW — In certain states, a law which requires that in the event a building is totally destroyed by fire, the company insuring it must pay the face amount of its policy irrespective of the actual value of the building destroyed.

VANDALISM — Damage done maliciously, included in the extended coverage endorsement. Also called "malicious mischief."

VENTURE — In ocean marine insurance, the undertaking, such as one voyage, of a vessel.

VOLUNTARY COMPENSATION COVERAGE — Protection which an employer may purchase to cover employees not otherwise included in the scope of workers compensation laws.

W

WAITING PERIOD — 1) In health insurance, the duration of time between the start of a disability and the start of benefits, as provided in the policy. Also known as ELIMINATION PERIOD. 2) In some business interruption insurance policies, a deductible clause.

WAIVER — 1) In property-liability insurance, the intentional relinquishment of a known right. To illustrate, an insurance policy may set forth certain conditions with which a policyholder must comply under penalty of voiding the insurance, e.g., maintain a watchman on the premises or keep a sprinkler system in working condition. The company may voluntarily give up this right to avoid the policy. Such a waiver may be conveyed by implication or by direct statement.

See ESTOPPEL, a term sometimes used interchangeably with waiver in the law of insurance. 2) A waiver-of-premium provision in a life or health insurance policy that the policy will be kept in force by the insurer without payment of further premiums if the insured becomes permanently and totally disabled as defined in the policy.

WAIVER OF SUBROGATION — A condition of an insurance policy which states that the coverage will not be prejudiced if the insured has waived in writing prior to a loss any rights of recovery from a party responsible for the loss.

WAR RISK CLAUSE — Language exempting the insurer from liability for claims arising out of war or warlike operations.

WAR RISK INSURANCE — Insurance against loss or damage to property due to war. It is freely written on marine risks but not on property on land. During World War II the government insured war risks on land.

WAREHOUSE-TO-WAREHOUSE CLAUSE — Language in a policy of marine cargo insurance which extends the protection from the warehouse at which the shipment originates to the one at which it terminates. Marine policies originally covered only on shipboard, leaving the property without insurance in between unless specifically arranged.

WAREHOUSEMAN'S LEGAL LIABILITY POLICY — Covers responsibility for loss or damage to property in the insured's warehouse.

WARRANTY — A statement by the insured on the literal truth of which the insurance contract depends. Warranties may relate to matters existing at or before the issuance of the policy (affirmative warranties) or may be undertakings by the insured that something be done or omitted after the policy takes effect and during its continuance (promissory warranties). Many states have restricted by statute the common law rule that "any breach of warranty avoids an insurance policy," e.g., under the New York law (150), a breach of warranty to avoid the policy must have "materially increased the risk of loss, damage or injury within the coverage of the contract."

WARSAW CONVENTION — An agreement reached in 1929 between a number of countries to establish uniform legislation affecting the legal responsibility of international air carriers. The convention (or laws enacted in conformity) limits the liability of air carriers of signatory countries to specify amounts for each passenger claim for bodily injury and also provides limits for damage to luggage or other cargo. This agreement relates only to international flights.

WATER DAMAGE INSURANCE — Insurance against loss due to the accidental presence of water (other than flood or surface water) in places it is not supposed to be.

WAVE DAMAGE INSURANCE — Insurance against damage done by the action of waves, as opposed to damage done by the wind alone. Wave damage is excluded by policies covering wind damage and must be insured by a special policy or clause attached to a policy.

WEDDING PRESENTS FLOATER — An "all-risks" inland marine form designed to insure wedding presents before and for a limited time after a wedding.

WINDSTORM (INCLUDING TORNADO & CYCLONE) INSURANCE — Protection against damage done to property by unusually high winds, cyclones, tornadoes, or hurricanes. Today windstorm insurance is not available except under an extended coverage endorsement.

WITHOUT PREJUDICE — An action taken during claims negotiations designated as "without prejudice" is intended to be without detriment to the existing rights of the parties. See NON-WAIVER AGREEMENT.

WORK AND MATERIALS CLAUSE — This clause gives the insured permission to perform those operations, and to keep on the premises those materials, which are usual to the occupancy of the insured. Standard fire insurance policies provide that they shall be suspended if the hazard is increased within the knowledge or control of the insured.

WORKERS COMPENSATION INSURANCE — Protection which provides benefits to employees for any injury or contracted disease arising out of and in the course of employment. All states have laws which require such protection for workers, and prescribe the length and amount of such benefits provided.

WRAP-UP POLICY — One policy, covering all involved interests for big construction projects; i.e., the owner, the contractor, subcontractor, suppliers, etc., providing general liability and workers compensation insurance.

WRITTEN PREMIUMS — The premiums on all the policies which a company has issued in a period of time, as opposed to EARNED PREMIUM.

Y

YACHT — A larger vessel used for pleasure purposes, as distinguished from a motorboat, sailboat, or commercial vessel.

YORK ANTWERP RULES — A set of rules adopted by the representatives of all the leading maritime nations to govern the method of applying GENERAL AVERAGE, revised in 1974.